IRELAND IN OLD PHOTOGRAPHS

CASTLEBAR

JOE CURTIS

First published 2013

The History Press Ireland
50 City Quay
Dublin 2
Ireland
www.thehistorypress.ie

© Joe Curtis, 2013

The right of Joe Curtis to be identified as the Author of this work has been asserted in accordance with the Copyrights, Designs and Patents Act 1988.

All rights reserved. No part of this book may be reprinted or reproduced or utilised in any form or by any electronic, mechanical or other means, now known or hereafter invented, including photocopying and recording, or in any information storage or retrieval system, without the permission in writing from the Publishers.

British Library Cataloguing in Publication Data.
A catalogue record for this book is available from the British Library.

ISBN 978 1 84588 790 2

Typesetting and origination by The History Press
Printed by TJ Books Limited, Padstow, Cornwall

CONTENTS

	Acknowledgements	4
1	Lord Lucan	5
2	Law and Order	17
3	Health	39
4	Religion and Education	63
5	Business	93
	Other Books by the Author	127

ACKNOWLEDGEMENTS

Grateful thanks to: Sr Cecilia Heslin (Ard Bhride, Castlebar), Sr Teresa Delaney (Mercy Archives, Galway), Br Oliver Rogers (De la Salle Archives), Edward Clarke (St Gerald's College), Ivor Hamrock (local history section of the County Library), Martin Cosgrove (Baxter Healthcare), Marie Crowley (Castlebar Town Clerk), Rose Doherty (Civil Defence), Revd Val Rogers (Christ Church), Trevor Ardill, Ivan Mohan and Anne Donnelly (both GMIT), Richard Gillespie (Roads Design in County Council), Tourist Office in Linenhall, Tom Kennedy (on behalf of Wynne family), Paul Ferguson (Trinity College Map Library), Nuala Armstrong, Hogs Heaven pub, Albany Decor, Joe Gilmore family and Western Alzheimers, McHugh family, Mary Fahey, Gavin family, Grace O'Malley, Mick Bohan, and all who allowed me to use photos, escorted me around their premises, told me their story, or assisted in numerous ways.

As usual, special thanks to the excellent staff at the National Library, National Archives, Irish Architectural Archive, Office of Public Works, Dublin City Archives and Gilbert Library, Valuation Office, and the Industrial Development Authority.

Many thanks to *Castlebar Parish Magazine*, especially Fr John Cosgrove PP, and Joe Redmond, its editor, for allowing me to reproduce some photos from various back editions, and thanks also to its contributing photographers, mostly local professionals, including those in the *Connaught Telegraph*.

Where photos are not acknowledged, they were taken by the author, mostly in 2012.

1

LORD LUCAN

Castlebar derives its name from 'Barry's castle', because the Norman family of de Barrie built a castle here in 1235. The Burke family acquired the property at a later date. The *Annals of the Four Masters* record that Caislean an Bharraigh was burned down in 1412 – it was probably a wooden structure – but there are further references to the castle in the *Annals* of 1576, and 1582.

The Bingham family came into possession of the land around 1584, and in 1613 King James I granted John Bingham a charter for the town of Castlebar. In the early eighteenth century, the Binghams built a small two-storey house near the original castle, calling it The Lawn House (sometimes called Castlebar House). The Binghams were not always in residence in The Lawn, as, for example, when St Clair O'Malley, land agent for the family, was recorded as being the occupier in the 1830s.

In 1795, Baron Charles Bingham was given the title Earl of Lucan, or Lord Lucan. Sir George Charles Bingham became notorious during the Famine in 1845-50 because of his cruel evictions. He was also infamous for foolishly leading his men to certain death during the Crimean War, in the 'Charge of the Light Brigade' at Balaclava in 1854. The family still lived in The Lawn in 1865, when Lord Lucan was the Lieutenant for Mayo. In 1888, the 4th Earl formally donated his cricket ground to the people of Castlebar, although the Green, or Mall, was never enclosed or walled-in.

In the 1901 Census, The Lawn was occupied by 72-year-old Archibald Bathgate, from Scotland, acting as steward. The house had eighteen rooms, while the extensive farm buildings totalled fifty-seven, including eight stables, eight cowhouses, thirteen piggeries, four barns, two fowlhouses, a forge, a corn mill, a saw mill, a kiln (for burning lime), and an engine house. Charles Weatherup occupied a smaller house, as assistant land agent.

In the 1911 Census, Fred Gahan from Donegal occupied The Lawn, and this time he lists eleven rooms. He is described as an inspector in the Congested Districts Board, and also a civil engineer.

The Lawn and extensive grounds were sold to the adjoining Sisters of Mercy in 1924. In 1974 the 7th Lord Lucan disappeared in London, and has never been found. Nowadays, some townspeople still pay ground rent to the Lucan Estate.

The Binghams are related to the Spencers, which was Lady Diana's family name. One of the Spencers was a judge in Castlebar, living in Spencer Park around 1900, which gave its name to Spencer Street. Lewis records a Major O'Malley living in Spencer Park in 1837.

Nowadays, there are no traces of the original Barry Castle, but it was obviously somewhere near Castle Street. Downing, writing in 1686, tells us that, 'next to Belcarra four miles distant stands Castle Barry, and has a large lawn and two round towers or castles.' Richard Pococke, in his book about a 1752 tour of Ireland, records that:

> This is the estate of Sir Charles Bingham, now abroad on his travels, who has a small house near the town, built on the site of an old castle after the revolution. The two large round towers of the old Castle remain, in which his grandfather lived with his Father-in-law Dr Vesey Archbishop of Tuam in King James' wars and defended themselves against the enemy.

During the Ordnance Survey of 1838, as recorded in Ordnance Survey letters (published in 1927), 'The site of the castle is pointed out in the yard of the new barracks, on a rising ground which is washed at its base by the River of Castlebar. A small portion of the foundations, from which the earth has been cleared away, can be seen.' The location of the former castle is marked clearly on the 1838 Ordnance Survey Town plan. Furthermore, in a survey of the bogs of Mayo in 1811, a map of Castlebar shows a Y-shaped building beside the river on the site where the barracks was later built in the 1830s, and this is probably the castle or a ruin.

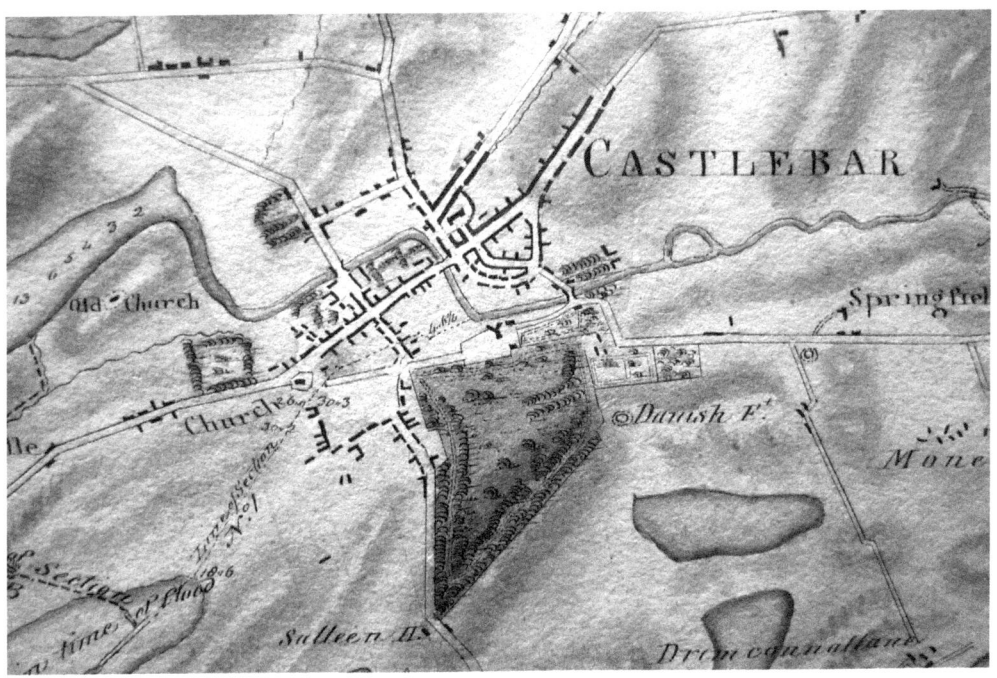

Castlebar in 1811. Note the Y-shaped building at the bend in the river, on the site of the present Army Barracks, which was probably the castle. (Courtesy of the National Library)

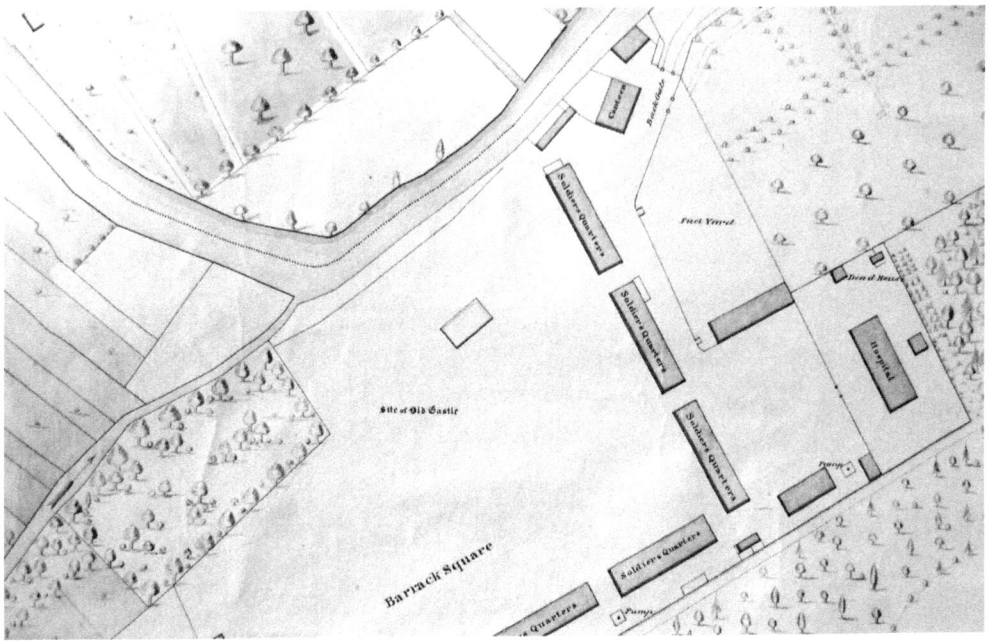

Ordnance Survey Town Plan of Castlebar, 1838. The 'Site of the Castle' is marked in the Army Barracks' square. Note the stream flowing from the direction of the Mall into the River Castlebar. (Courtesy of the National Archives)

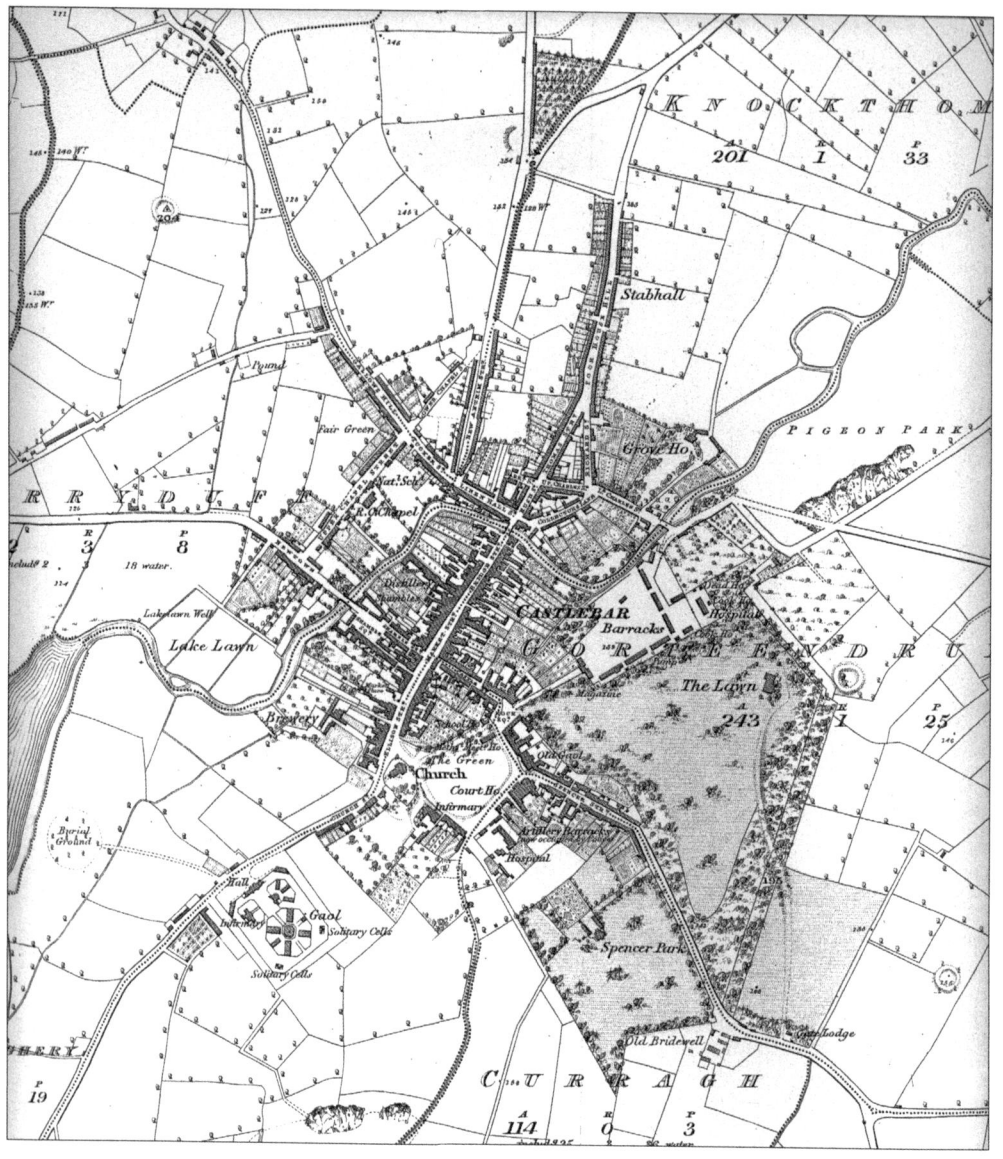

Ordnance Survey map of Castlebar, 1838. (Courtesy of Trinity College, Dublin – Map Library)

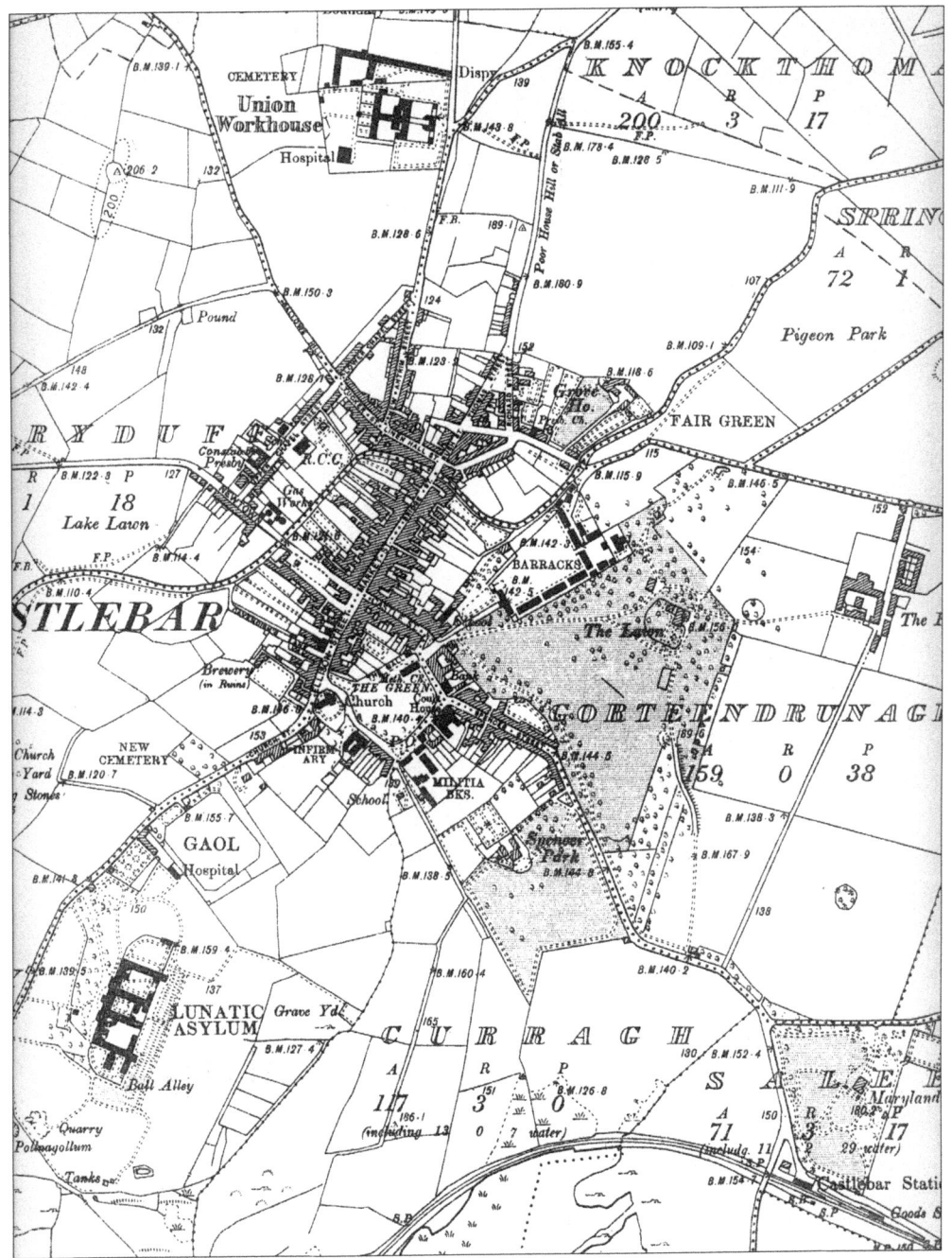

Ordnance Survey map of Castlebar, 1895/96. The gaol buildings are not shown, possibly for security reasons. Note the farm in the centre right, which later became the Bacon Factory. (Courtesy of Trinity College, Dublin – Map Library)

The Lawn, *c.* 1900. This was the seat of the Binghams (Lord Lucan), after the Cromwellian wars, and is now part of St Joseph's Secondary School. (Courtesy of the National Library – Lawrence Collection)

This cartoon, entitled 'The Castlebar Races, August 27th 1798', was included in the Christmas 1887 edition of *The Shamrock*. (Courtesy of the National Library)

THE RACES OF CASTLEBAR

'The Races of Castlebar' refers to the 1798 rebellion in Ireland against the British occupation. General Humbert, with a small French force, landed on 22 August 1798 at Kilcummin Strand, north of Killala, and teamed up with an Irish contingent. When they reached Castlebar on 27 August, they routed the British garrison, who 'raced off' towards the Midlands. However, on 8 September 1798, the Franco-Irish forces were surrounded at Ballinamuck, Co. Longford. Here they were forced to surrender, and although the French were allowed to return to France, the Irish were slaughtered.

Meanwhile, John Moore (from Moore Hall beside Lough Carra) had been pronounced President of the Republic of Connaught, as the local representative of the United Irishmen. After the defeat of the Franco-Irish forces in Longford, John Moore was being transported to Britain, but died before he got there and was buried in Waterford in 1799.

On the road about two miles south of Castlebar, there is a stone obelisk remembering the Races of Castlebar. The plaque reads: 'In grateful remembrance of the gallant French soldiers who died fighting for the freedom of Ireland on the 27th August 1798. They shall be remembered for ever. Erected 1876.' The *Irish Sword* magazine recorded a visit there in 1905, noting three graves of French officers, two of which were marked with small iron crosses. One grave was partially open at the side, and part of a rusty sword could be seen.

Commemorations were held in Castlebar in 1948 for the 150th anniversary of the 1798 rebellion, including Mass, a pageant re-enacting the Races, and a military exhibition, centred around the Barracks, with the FCA (army reserve force) being heavily involved. In 1953, the present memorial was erected on The Mall, opposite Christ Church.

On 13 August 1961, John Moore's body was removed from Waterford and re-interred beside the 1798 Monument on The Mall in Castlebar – with full military honours – in the presence of President Eamon de Valera and Taoiseach Sean Lemass.

In the graveyard attached to Christ Church, there is a headstone for six named soldiers of the Fraser Highlanders (from Scotland) who died in the Races.

Now that the 1916 centenary commemorations are not far off, wouldn't it be wonderful to move the obelisk and graves from French Hill to their rightful place on The Mall.

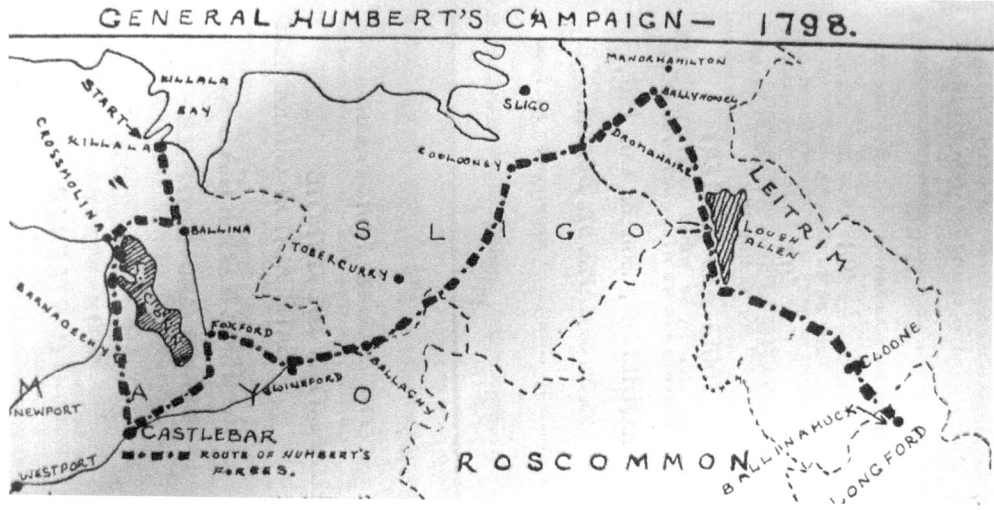

This sketch was included in a 1948 booklet, commemorating the 1798 Rising. (Courtesy of Dublin City Archives)

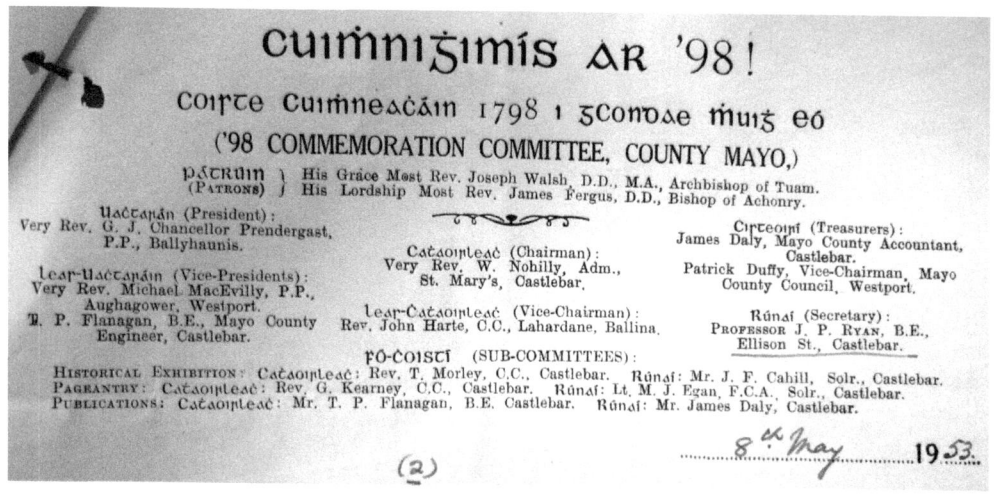

The 1948 commemorations concluded with the erection of a monument in The Mall in 1953. Note the heavy Church involvement in the organising committee. (Courtesy of the National Archives)

President Sean T. O'Ceallaigh inspecting the Guard of Honour outside the Church of the Holy Rosary in Castlebar, during the 1948 commemorations. (Courtesy of *Castlebar Parish Magazine*)

The 1961 re-burial of John Moore, first President of Connaught, in The Mall beside the 1798 Monument. Here, the gun carriage carrying the coffin, and draped with the Irish tricolour, is escorted by army officers. (Courtesy of the *Connaught Telegraph*)

Another photograph of the 1961 re-burial of John Moore. Here the coffin leaves the Church of the Holy Rosary, with President Eamon de Valera and Taoiseach Sean Lemass visible on the right. (Courtesy of the *Connaught Telegraph*)

The east face of the 1798 monument on The Mall. The Irish inscription reads: '*A Mhuire na nGael guidh orainn*', meaning, 'Mary of the Irish, pray for us'. The other face has the inscription: '*i gCuimhe* 1798', meaning, 'In memory of 1798'. In the background, note the General George O'Malley monument behind the railings of Christ Church.

Castlebar during the 1948 commemorations of the 1798 Rising, when French flags were flown from every building. (Courtesy of *Castlebar Parish Magazine*)

The Mall in 2012. John Moore's grave (left) dates from 1961, while the 1798 monument (right) dates from 1953.

Moore Hall, home of the first President of Connaught, has lain in ruins for ninety years, after being set on fire in February 1923 during the Civil War.

The 1798 monument/obelisk on French Hill, on the road to Belcarra, 2012. It was erected in 1876, and originally had a metal cross on top. This is on private property, with no public access, and is hidden behind new housing.

2

LAW AND ORDER

CASTLEBAR INFANTRY BARRACKS

Castlebar was a garrison town since 1691 and the Infantry Barracks was built there in 1834 on a 6½ acre site beside The Lawn. The barracks could hold 1,000 men, and Irish soldiers were mostly stationed here, especially the Connaught Rangers, who were well liked around the town. Around 1916, the Munster Fusiliers were stationed here, but after 1918 British troops were drafted in, such as the Border Regiment.

An army map of 1865 (corrected in 1883) records accommodation for 246 privates and non-commissioned officers, twenty officers, two staff sergeants, twenty-six hospital patients, two field officers, and six horses. There were six blocks, all three-storeys high: four for soldiers and two for officers, the latter having three staircases in each. There was also a two-storey hospital in the south-east corner, and a two-storey canteen in the north-east corner, near the Grove Bridge entrance.

Internal lighting was by candles, and external lighting by oil; heating was by means of open fireplaces in each dormitory or room; dry earth closets (toilets) and urinals were positioned separately alongside boundary walls; the magazine, which contained ammunitions and gun powder, was located to the south of the entrance archway; a school room was located on the first floor of Block B; and the handball alley was at the north-west, against which the Mercy nuns built St Joseph's grotto. The adjoining river is marked as the River Lannagh, since the river flowed eastwards out of this nearby lake and a tributary stream flowed from the rear of the nuns' adjoining property into the main river.

On 9 February 1916, the south-eastern portion of the Barracks (Block E/F and Cook House) was handed over to the Royal Irish Constabulary (RIC), on the instructions of the British War Office. The RIC then moved to the vacated gaol in November 1919.

During the Civil War in 1922, the former empty RIC block in the Army Barracks was set on fire and partially damaged. After Independence, the various blocks were modernised and altered, and a new dining hall/mess built in 1928. Alterations included the addition of outrigger toilets to the rear elevations of the soldiers' blocks, the removal of one staircase from each of the two officers' blocks, and the installation of front porches. In the 1950s and '60s, the detached dining hall was used by the soldiers for playing basketball, and also for public concerts. Also in that era, the annual carnival in Castlebar was set up in the barracks' square.

In the 1960s, Block A/B was used by the Planning Department of Mayo County Council, Block C/D was used by the Department of Agriculture, and Block G/H was used as St Patrick's Boys National School after a fire in the school in Chapel Street. In recent decades, the reserve army (the FCA) has used part of the Barracks. Regrettably, Block E/F and Block J/K/L were demolished during this period.

In 2012, the County Council and Town Council acquired the Barracks, and there is now a great opportunity to carry out an archaeological dig to search for the foundations of the original castle in the open square. As the Barracks is a Protected Structure, its future is guaranteed, and there are high hopes for a major cultural amenity.

CASTLEBAR CAVALRY BARRACKS

Castlebar Cavalry Barracks was on the site of the present-day Garda Divisional Headquarters, built in 1995; all that remains of the Old Barracks are the two statues of lions outside the entrance. Dr Richard Pococke, in his 1752 tour of Ireland, records, 'It is a pretty good small town, having a good market and a Horse Barrack.' The map produced by the British War Office in 1865 shows a small number of buildings – some single-storey and others two-storey – including stabling for the horses. At that time, there was accommodation for three officers, two sergeants, forty-three privates and non-commissioned officers, six horses for officers, and thirty-seven horses for troops. By deed, dated 12 August 1910, the barracks was sold to the Congested Districts Board for £600. They only occupied the small two-storey central block, while the Inland Revenue occupied the larger two-storey U-shaped block.

THE ROYAL IRISH CONSTABULARY (RIC)

The RIC occupied different buildings in Castlebar over the years, including two adjoining houses near the presbytery in Chapel Street for the second half of the nineteenth century. In the 1901 Census, the RIC were in Ellison Street (now called Chambers House), to the left of the National Bank, with rear access off Cavendish Lane. It comprised of a head constable, three sergeants, and ten constables. The head constable was Church of Ireland, one sergeant and one constable were Presbyterian, and the other eleven were Catholics. By 1911 the staff had been reduced by two sergeants. The RIC moved to Block E/F in the Infantry Barracks in 1916, and the empty Ellison Street premises was set on fire by the IRA in 1920. In 1919 the RIC moved into the closed gaol. After the Civil War in 1922/23, the RIC was disbanded and the new Garda Síochána came into being, initially headquartered in Swinford.

From the mid-1930s, the Gardaí occupied the former Cavalry Barracks beside the Courthouse, although shared the complex with other government agencies, including the Land Commission, Department of Posts and Telegraphs, Department of Social Welfare, and regional architects division of the Office of Public Works. Records show that, in 1965, there were six sergeants and twenty-two Gardaí based here. It is interesting to note in the 1838 Town Plan that the police were in occupation of the former Cavalry Barracks and they enjoyed the use of a large rear garden.

THE COURTHOUSE

The Courthouse on the Mall, designed by George Papworth, dates from 1822 and was called the Session House. In 1860 additions and alterations were carried out by architect George Wilkinson, including adding an extra storey on to both wings, and adding a portico (as envisaged by Papworth) with columns made from cast iron, instead of the more usual stone. The extended building had two court rooms, one the Record Court, and the other the Crown Court. The 1901 census lists Mr Gallagher and family as Court Keepers. In 2004, a large rear extension was added, and the original courts were partially re-modelled, so that the complex now has four courtrooms, with the usual ancillary facilities. However, Court No. 2 still retains much of its original layout and furnishings, including the cast-iron columns supporting the gallery, inscribed with the name 'J. Stephens, Galway'.

COUNTY GAOL

There was a small gaol on the Mall, on the site where the Bank of Ireland later built its premises. The Grand Jury (local government) took possession of the old gaol in 1781, stating that a military guard was necessary to protect the gaol, since there was no army in the whole of the county. A report of 1823 states that the gaol held 180, with two prisoners per bed, and the Bridewell attached to the Courthouse held forty-six. Prior to its closure in 1834, prisoners were eighteen to a cell.

The new County Gaol was on the Westport Road, on the site of the present Mayo General Hospital. It was built in 1834, to a design by Frederick Darley, and had a central block, comprising the Governor's House, with a chapel on the second floor, and then four wings radiating from the centre; each three storeys high, with a total capacity of 128 single cells. There was also a treadmill for raising water from a well. By the time the property was surveyed in the 1920s some wings had been demolished.

The Parliamentary Gazetteer of Ireland records that, in 1840, there were twenty-six females, twenty working and six engaged on prison duties. There were ninety-six males, forty-four at useful trades, nineteen at stone-breaking, twenty-six at the tread wheel, and nine on prison duties. At Christmas 1842, there were forty-five male debtors, one female debtor, one-hundred-and-five male criminals, seventeen untried male criminals, twenty-two female criminals, twelve untried female criminals, six in hospital, two male lunatics, and three female lunatics. In a government report of 1844, there were fifty-seven men, nineteen women, thirty-five debtors, and seventeen lunatics. Reference is made to an infirmary, well-divided chapel, laundry, public kitchen, school run by a turnkey (warder), and work at stone-breaking and on the tread-wheel.

In 1850, at a time when the workhouse held nearly 2,000 people, the gaol held 434 prisoners – which was regarded as more than double the usual capacity – as a result of destitute people opting for gaol. Breakfast consisted of 8 ounces of oatmeal porridge and 1 pint of buttermilk, while dinner was 14 ounces white bread and 1 pint of sweet-milk. The governor, D.R. Young, received £200 per year, the turnkeys got £30, and Protestant Chaplin Revd Stoney and Catholic Chaplin Revd J. McHale each got £37 10s.

The prison closed on 6 November 1919, and five days later was handed over to the RIC, a portion being reserved by the police for temporary accommodation of prisoners and prison officers at Castlebar Assizes and Quarter Sessions (court hearings).

In July and August 1922, the RIC Barracks was damaged and looted to the tune of £9,000, after which the Saorstat (Free State) army went into occupation until 1927. The former gaol was handed over to the County Council in July 1929, demolished in 1932, and the County Hospital built on the site in 1938.

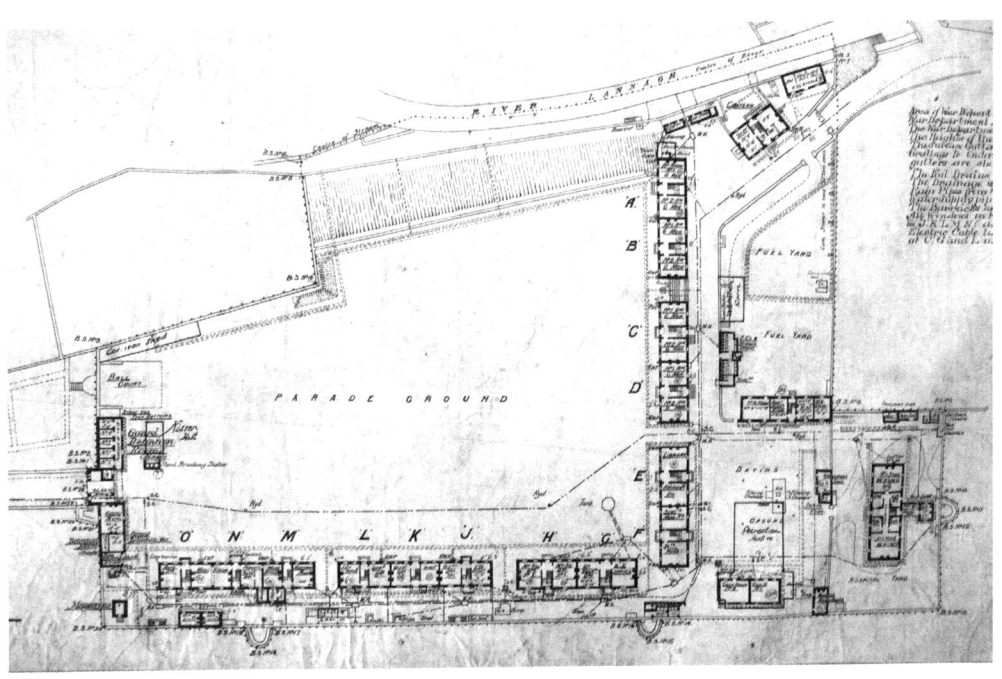

1917 map of Castlebar Infantry Barracks. (Courtesy of the Office of Public Works)

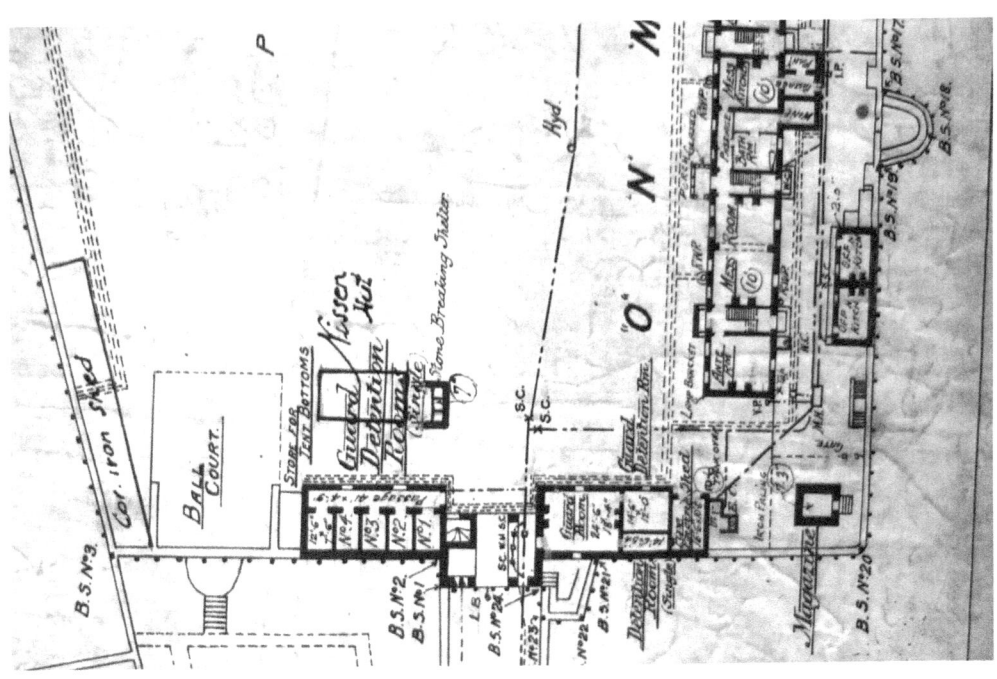

Close-up of a 1917 map of Castlebar Infantry Barracks. At the bottom is the entrance archway, including prison cells, and to the right is an Officer's Block. The magazine (gun powder) is at bottom right. Note what appears to be a semi-circular watchtower in the boundary wall on the right. (Courtesy of the Office of Public Works)

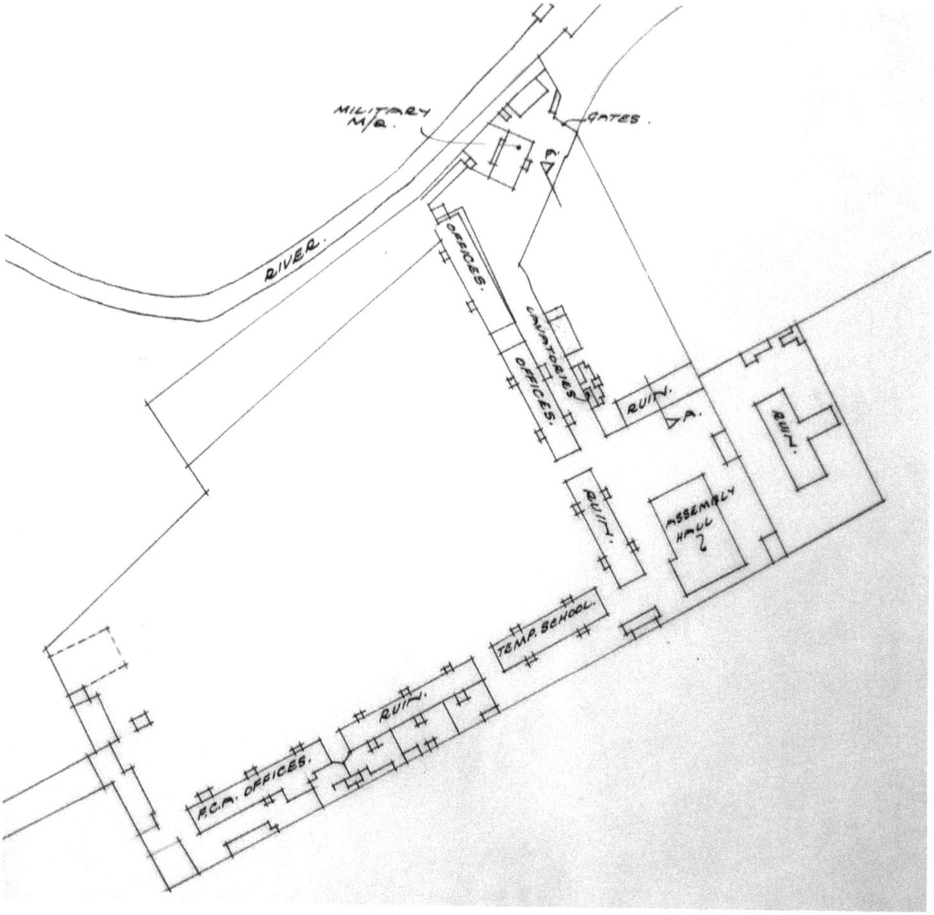

1960s map of the Army Barracks, with the FCA (army reserve force) block on the lower left, followed by a ruin, a temporary school, another ruin, then two blocks of offices. The original canteen beside the back gate is shown as 'Military Married Quarters'. The former hospital, behind the 1928 hall/mess at the lower right, is also a ruin. (Courtesy of Office of the Public Works)

Current view of the Army Barracks, with Soldiers' Block E/F gone, and Officers' Block J/K/L replaced by prefabs. Block E/F was occupied by the RIC from 1916 to 1919.

The prefabs on the left are a replacement for Officers' Block J/K/L.

The magazine is still in the south-west corner of the Army Barracks.

Rear view of Block A/B. This block, and the former canteen beside the rear gate, are the only ones to have basements. The rear outrigger toilets were added in the 1920s.

The FCA (army reserve force) in Castlebar in this 1999 photo of sergeants from all over Connaught. (Photograph by Heverin Photography and supplied by Grace O'Malley)

One-hundred-strong Presidential Guard of Honour lining-up in Castlebar Barracks in 1988, for the visit of President Hillery, comprising 5th Cavalry Squadron and 18th Infantry Battalion personnel. (Courtesy of Captain Mick Bohan, OC, 54 Reserve Cavalry Squadron)

FCA outside Block D in Castlebar Barracks. (Courtesy of Captain Mick Bohan, OC, 54 Reserve Cavalry Squadron)

Chaplain Fr Shannon with the FCA, *c.* 1970. (Courtesy of Captain Mick Bohan, OC, 54 Reserve Cavalry Squadron)

Castlebar Barracks, with the dining hall in the background, and the ruin of the hospital just visible. Pictured are the 5th Motor Squadron, combined weapons winners of 1962/63. (Courtesy of Captain Mick Bohan, OC, 54 Reserve Cavalry Squadron)

Infantry FCA marching down McHale Road, *c.* 1956/57, in the St Patrick's Day Parade. The Bacon Factory is just about visible in the distance. (Courtesy of Captain Mick Bohan, OC, 54 Reserve Cavalry Squadron)

In the 1950s and 1960s, the carnival set up in the Army Barracks. (Wynne Family Collection)

A fair in the Army Barracks in the 1950s. (Wynne Family Collection)

The centre of this aerial photograph shows the south-west corner of The Mall, or Green, especially the old Garda station (the long U-shaped building), which was formerly a Cavalry Barracks. Soprano Margaret Burke Sheridan lived in the three-storey former post office beside the north-east corner of the Barracks. The vacant site to the left of the Garda station is now the County Library. (Courtesy of Roads Design, Mayo County Council)

A pair of lions from the former Cavalry Barracks now guard the Garda station.

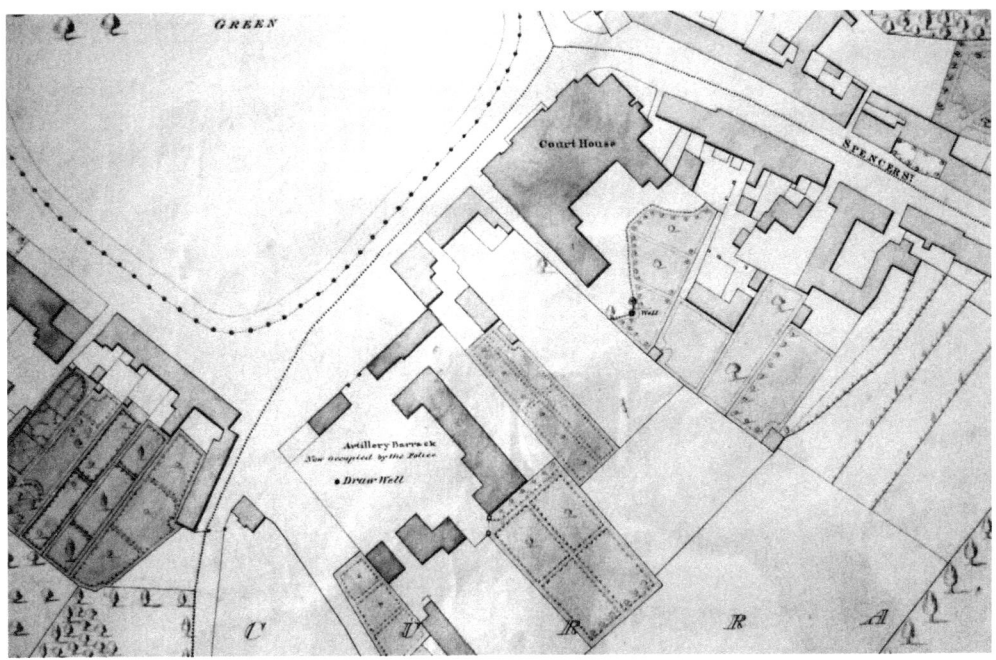

1838 map showing the Artillery Barracks (also known as the Cavalry Barracks) on The Mall, which were used by the police back then. The perimeter buildings were single storey, while the two central buildings were two-storey. It is now the site of the Garda station. (Courtesy of the National Archives)

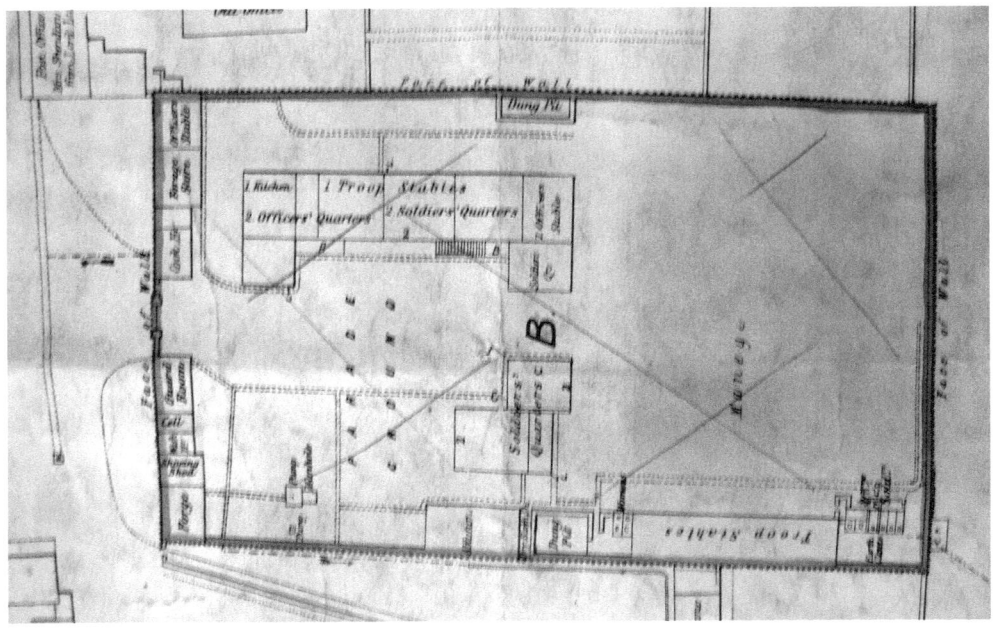

1883 map of Artillery/Cavalry Barracks on The Mall. The post office at the top left is shown as leased by Mrs Sheridan. (Courtesy of the Bureau of Military Archives)

1933 map of the Artillery (or Cavalry) Barracks, now owned by the Land Commission. The Inland Revenue were housed in the U-shaped block at the time. (Courtesy of the Office of Public Works)

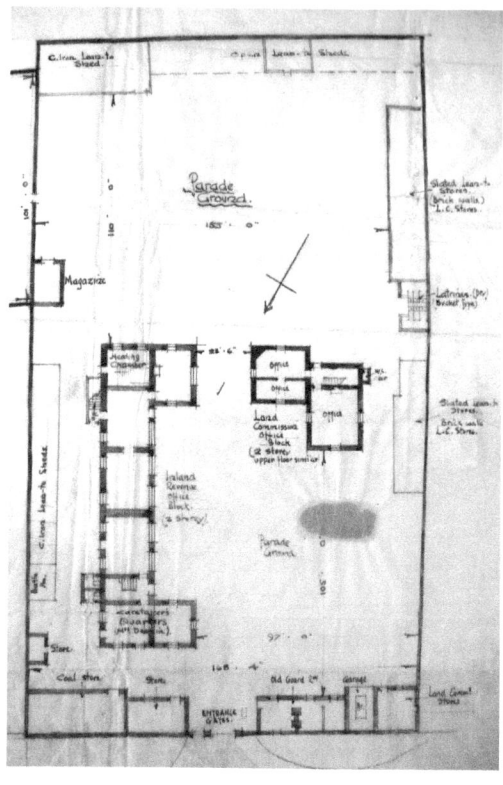

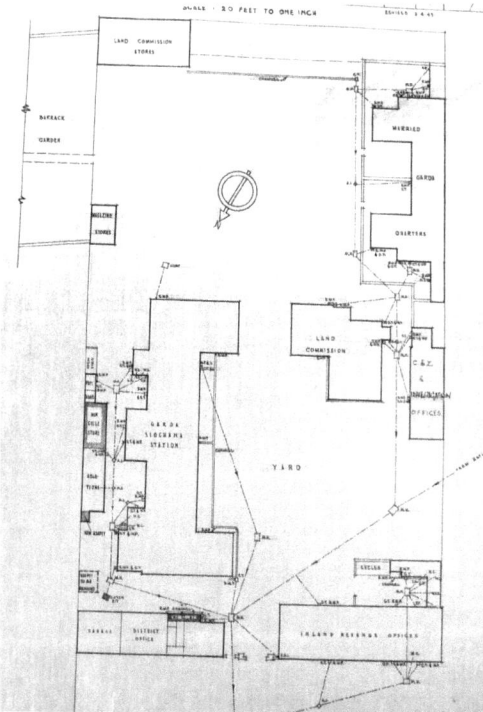

1936 map of the former Artillery (or Cavalry) Barracks on The Mall. The main two-storey, U-shaped building, near the lower left, was the Garda station (previously the Inland Revenue), and their married quarters were in the converted single-storey stables, at the top right. The Land Commission were in the small central two-storey building. (Courtesy of the Office of Public Works)

Prior to the new building opening in 1995, the Gardaí occupied a converted building on the same site of the former Artillery (or Cavalry) Barracks on The Mall. (Courtesy of Garda Síochána – presented by Paul Heverin Photography in 1993, and now displayed in the foyer of the Garda station)

Gardaí in their old station on The Mall in 1974 (on the same site as the present 1995 building). (Courtesy of the *Connaught Telegraph*)

Gardaí in Castlebar, 1960. (Courtesy of *Castlebar Parish Magazine*)

The Courthouse on The Mall/Green, *c.* 1900. Note the low-level Artillery (or Cavalry) Barracks to the left of the tree trunk. (Courtesy of the National Library – Lawrence Collection)

The Courthouse recently underwent a major extension and refurbishment. However, Court No. 2, at the front left-hand side, still retains most of its original character.

The refurbished Court No. 2.

The gaol, *c.* 1880. It is now the site of Mayo General Hospital. (Courtesy of the National Library – Wynne Collection)

The main entrance and clock tower to the gaol, *c.* 1900. (Courtesy of the National Library – Lawrence Collection)

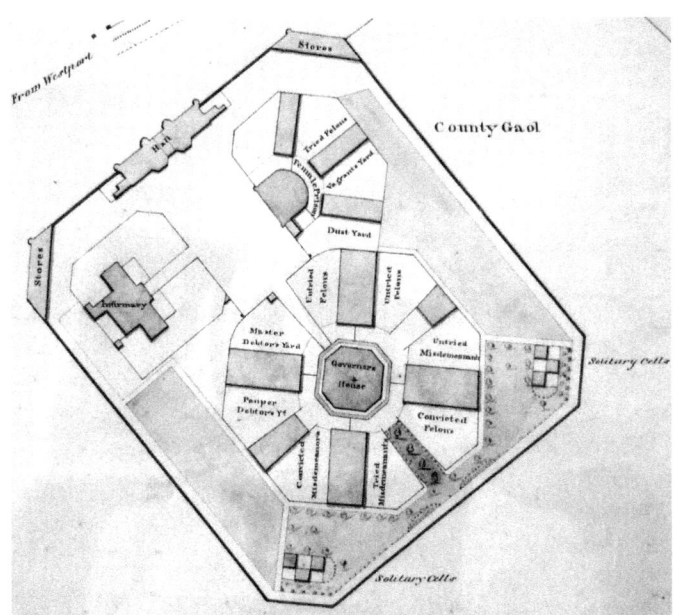

The gaol shown on an 1838 Castlebar Town plan. The Governor's House is in the centre of the octagonal range of buildings. (Courtesy of the National Archives)

The Governor's House in the gaol in 1920; the top floor was a chapel. (Courtesy of the National Archives)

The Governor's House in the gaol in 1920. (Courtesy of the National Archives)

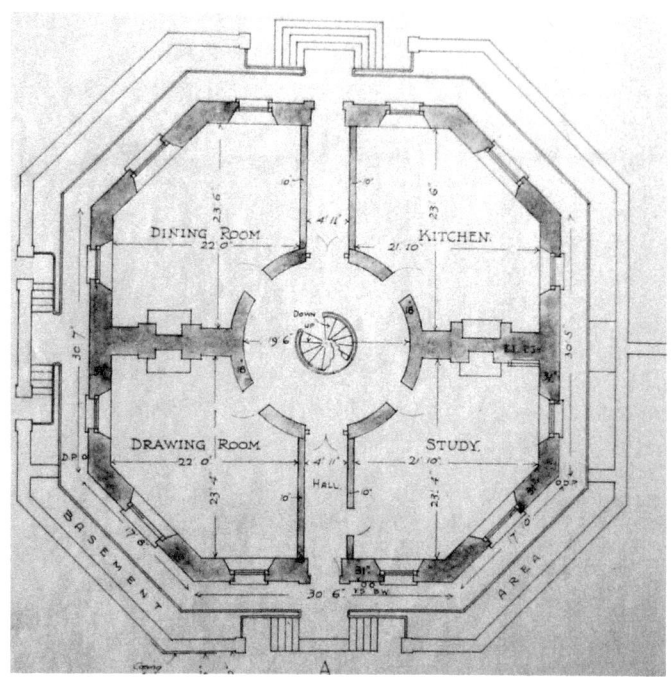

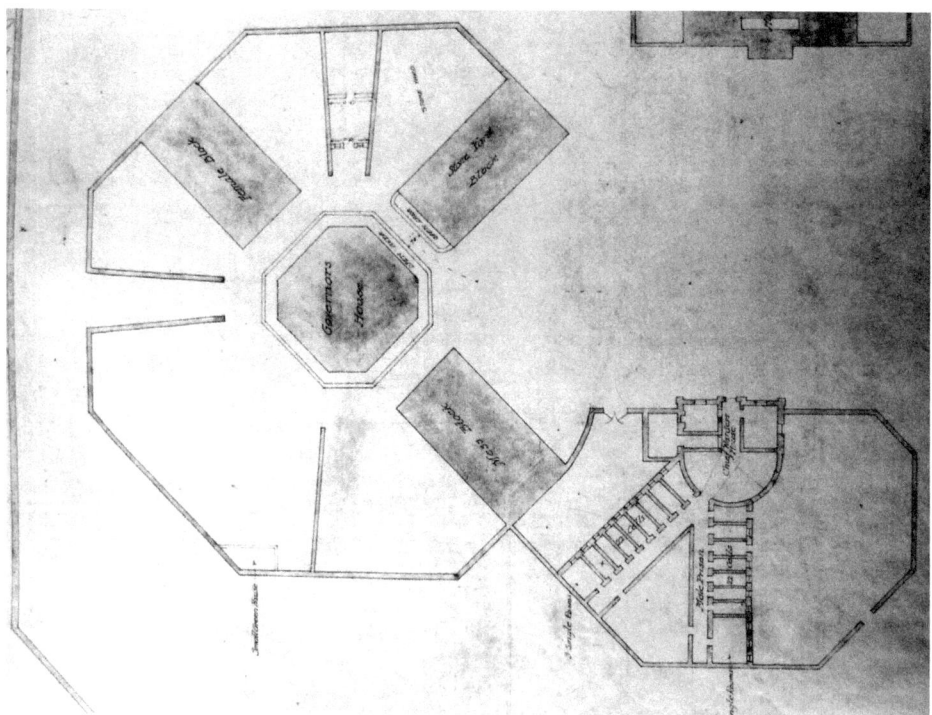

The gaol in 1920, comprising the Governor's House, female block, mess block, and stone yard block, with a male prison (forty-four cells over three floors) and chief warder's house at lower right. The hospital is shown at the top right-hand corner. (Courtesy of the National Archives)

LOCAL GOVERNMENT

Prior to an Act of 1898, local government was in the hands of the Grand Jury, who met a few times every year in the Courthouse on The Mall. Mayo County Council held its first elections on 6 April 1899 and for many decades held its meetings in the Courthouse, as did Castlebar Urban Council.

The former Linen Hall came into the possession of the Catholic Church around 1898 for use as a social centre, and was known as the Town Hall, although had nothing to do with local government. Soon after that, the parish priest organised the building of a concert hall behind the original building.

An official Coat of Arms was granted to Castlebar in 1953 by the Chief Herald of Ireland, and comprises a castle, two yew trees (representing the county of Maigh Eo – plain of the yew trees), two pikes (in memory of the Races of Castlebar), five crosses (symbolising the Catholic parish of Agish), and the words '*Ar Aghaidh*' (Irish for 'forward').

Present council chamber, Mayo County Council, The Mall, Castlebar. There is a plaque on the wall commemorating Sean Corcoran from Kiltimagh, who died in the War of Independence in 1921.

Marsh House, Newtown, current headquarters of Castlebar Urban Council. This was the former home of Sr Gertrude (Mary Feeney), who entered the Mercy Convent in Castlebar in 1860.

Castlebar Fire Brigade, 1970. (Courtesy of *Castlebar Parish Magazine*)

3

HEALTH

There was an infirmary on the west side of the Mall, from 1834 to 1938. In 1846 there were forty-seven beds, and by the time of the 1901 census there were thirty-one patients, including children, and eleven staff. In the 1911 census, there were thirty-seven patients. The site is now occupied by the County Council headquarters, built in 1989.

The present modern General Hospital on the Westport Road has capacity for 320 beds, and has 1,300 staff. It was built on the site of the gaol, demolished in 1932, and opened in 1938. The foundation stone of a large extension was laid in 1986, and another phase built in the 1990s.

MAYO LUNATIC ASYLUM

The Mayo Lunatic Asylum on the Westport Road, which was designed by George Wilkinson, opened in 1865. It was subsequently extended a few times (the north wing in 1936 was the last) and the detached chapel was built in 1903. The layout comprised rows of cells, in addition to some dormitories. The 1901 Census recorded 663 people on the premises, including a lot of attendants and many young nurses. Quite a large number of the patients had dementia, which nowadays is treated in ordinary nursing homes. In the 1911 Census, numbers had increased to 862, including those in the fever hospital. The asylum was called St Mary's Psychiatric Hospital in the 1950s, and the high walls surrounding the hospital were demolished in the early 1960s.

There was a large farm as part of the asylum. It was worked by the patients and supplied many of their own needs, such as milk and vegetables, with the excess output sold in the town. The initial farm was about 50 acres, but increased to about 250 acres in various locations around Castlebar.

The patients also made all their own clothes and shoes, and there was a running track and football field at the rear of the asylum, which were put to good use at the annual Sports Day, when all of Castlebar descended on the asylum.

The iconic clock tower now has a digital clock, replacing the original 1866 Benson two-train hand-wound clock. However, the new clock still strikes the hour on the big bell, cast in 1866 by Mears and Stainbank of London (now the famous Whitechapel Foundry).

The asylum had its own cemetery, some distance to the east of the site, which was in use until the founding of the new State in 1922. After that date, patients were buried in a mass grave in the old town cemetery, without any religious blessing or headstone. When the new Castlebar inner-relief road was completed in 1992, the original asylum cemetery was cut-off across the road from the new fire brigade station. However, in 2005 it was officially re-opened as Castlebar Peace Park, and a basic headstone erected. It also contains the mass grave of the many civilians who died of the Spanish flu after the First World War.

In 1994, the Galway-Mayo Institute of Technology (GMIT) took over one wing of the hospital and nicely converted it into a third-level college. Over the years they acquired most of the remainder of the old hospital, which eventually closed in 2006, although the north block is still used by the HSE as an administration centre. One 1972 building at the south end of the campus was retained for St Teresa's Psychiatric Unit, with forty beds.

SACRED HEART HOSPITAL

The Sacred Heart Hospital on the Pontoon Road, until recently run by the Sisters of Mercy, specialises in geriatrics. It was extended in 2010 and can now accommodate 300 patients. This hospital was formerly called the County Home and converted from the Union Workhouse (Poor Law Union) in 1922 by the County Board of Health, although still very basic. Three Sisters of Mercy nuns were sent from Castlebar Convent to Cork to train as nurses, and after three years were employed to run the County Home. Around the end of the 1920s, small extensions were built for toilets, and a new drainage scheme installed – before that, outside privies were used. The present Sacred Heart Hospital dates from 1973, and the workhouse was demolished in 1971. No one remembers the overgrown cemetery at the rear, containing thousands of bodies, since there is not even one headstone or plaque.

About 350 Workhouses were built in England and Wales in the 1830s as a last refuge for poor and destitute people, and the scheme was extended to Ireland after an Act of 1838. These institutions were semi-prisons in nature and the occupants were expected to work for their keep, doing domestic chores, and even stone-breaking.

The English architect, George Wilkinson, was responsible for the design of all 130 Workhouses in Ireland (more were built after the Famine), using a standard design for all of them. Castlebar Workhouse was opened in 1842, built at a total cost of £7,949 on an 7-acre site bought for £340. It comprised of a small front block for administration (two probationary wards with a bath on the ground floor, and a boardroom on the first floor) and a much larger central block to accommodate about 600 people (officially revised later to 840), with separate divisions for girls, boys, women, and men. This main block was two storeys, although the dormitory wings at each end were three storeys. At right-angles to the rear centre of the main building was the single-storey chapel-cum-dining room. Beyond the main block was another two-storey building, including an infirmary and wards for 'idiots'. There was also a small, detached two-storey fever hospital, which was later supplemented with fever sheds.

In 1847 it is recorded that there were only 401 paupers present in the Workhouse. However, by 1850, 3½ acres of extra land had been acquired adjoining the north side of the workhouse, and two auxiliary workhouses had been built, with a combined extra capacity of 600 (the F-shaped range on the plan on p.56), and another one was proposed. A cemetery was positioned at the west end of this new site. The Guardians secured a loan of £1,000 for the extra buildings. In addition, records refer to the hire of Walshe's Brewery to accommodate 332 women, and another hired building to accommodate 130 (the brewery site is now occupied by new shops between Hopkins Road and the multi-storey car park). Therefore, in 1850, the overall Workhouse capacity was 1,952, nearly three times the original plans. By 1866, the four auxiliary workhouses were not in use, and capacity of the original workhouse was down to about 750. In 1877, the average number of occupants was 110.

In the 1911 Census, there were eighty-four patients present, in addition to eight 'lunatics'. Charles Ryan is listed as the master, Mary Tierney the school teacher, Mary Cleary the matron, and James Corley the porter.

Although the Workhouse in Castlebar is gone, we know from other existing buildings elsewhere in Ireland something about the standard of accommodation. The interior walls were not plastered, but were whitewashed with lime, which was regarded as a disinfectant; the ground floor was initially compacted bare clay, but later improved with flagstones; the first floor had bare floorboards, with no plaster on the underside; and the upper wards had no ceilings, so that the roof structure was visible – queen-post trusses in the main spaces, and basic collar roofs in the end wings. In winter time, all that separated the occupants of the upper floors from the wind, rain and snow outside, was a thin slate. In the two end wings, a narrow limestone staircase linked the floors. The exterior was built with rough grey limestone, and the timber windows had iron glazing bars to create a diamond pattern. Heating in winter was by means of a few turf fires, although there were none in the end dormitory wings. The occupants effectively slept on the bare timber floor, on a basic mattress of straw – a central gangway ran down the middle of each dormitory, about eight inches below the main floor, as a means of access. Inmates were provided with a type of uniform, made by the Castlebar Industrial Society.

Food usage in the Infirmary, Castlebar, 1903. The main items were bread, potatoes, milk, meat, butter, tea, sugar, bacon, salt, eggs, whiskey, brandy, and soap. (Courtesy of the National Library)

The Infirmary, to the left of Christ Church, c. 1900. It is now the site of Mayo County Council headquarters. (Courtesy of the National Library – Lawrence Collection)

The County Hospital, which was built in 1938 on the site of the old gaol. It is now part of the much larger Mayo General Hospital. (Courtesy of the National Library)

County Hospital, 1940s. (Courtesy of the National Library)

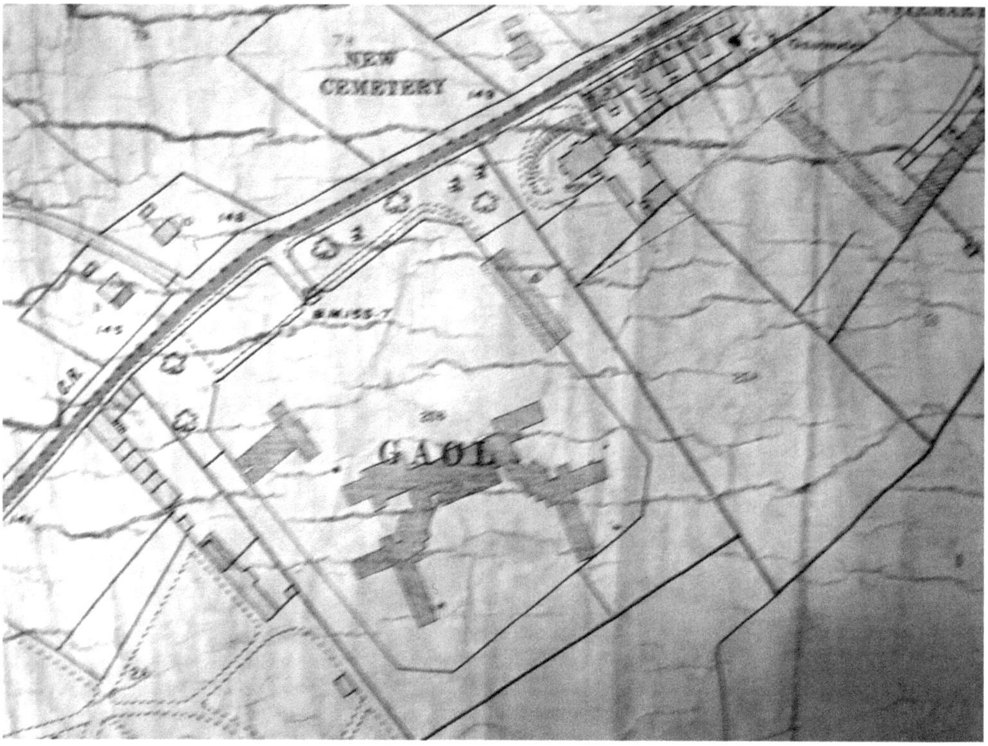

Ordnance Survey map of the new County Hospital on the former gaol site. (Courtesy of the Valuation Office)

The 1938 buildings are still part of the larger Mayo General Hospital.

St Mary's Psychiatric Hospital, with a detached chapel at bottom of photo. It is now Galway-Mayo Institute of Technology. (Courtesy of GMIT – *Snapshots in Time*)

St Mary's Psychiatric Hospital. Note Mayo General Hospital at the top of the photo. (Courtesy of GMIT)

Above Mayo Lunatic Asylum in the 1880s. (Wynne Family Collection)

Present view of St Mary's Psychiatric Hospital. (Courtesy of GMIT)

Another present-day view of St Mary's. (Courtesy of GMIT)

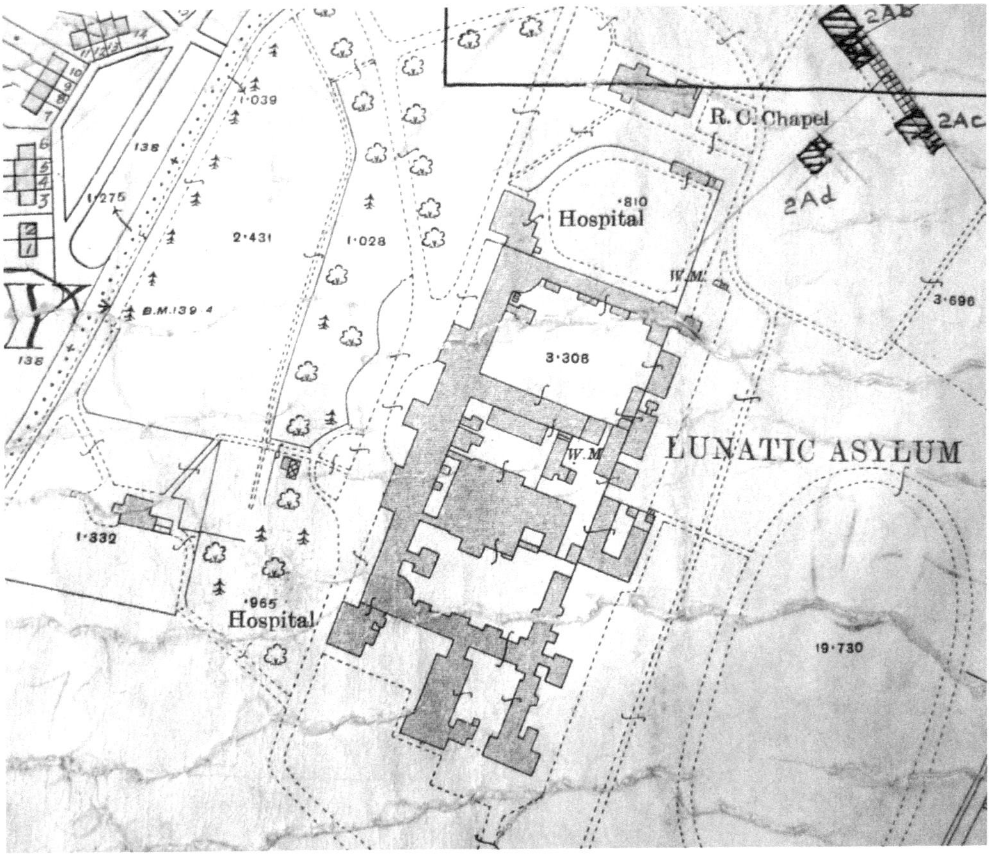

Mayo Lunatic Asylum in the 1920s, before being extended. (Courtesy of the Valuation Office)

Public Sports Day at Mayo Lunatic Asylum in the 1930s, centred around the rear running track and football pitch. (Courtesy of St Mary's/GMIT)

PROGRAMME

OF GRAND

TOURNAMENT

AND

MILITARY FETE

TO BE HELD IN THE

ASYLUM SPORTS GROUND, CASTLEBAR,

On SUNDAY, 12th JULY, 1914,

Under the Auspices of Castlebar Battalion Irish National Volunteers.

OFFICERS:

John Hoban, President; John McGowan, Treasurer; Andrew Ryan, Secretary; M. J. Short, Officer Commanding Castlebar Battalion.

COMMITTEE:

P. Concannon, P. Monnelly, H. Dupree, P. McCormack, M. J. Egan, J. Fogarty, U.D.C.; J. Hughes, M. McHugh, T. J. Loftus, J.P., U.D.C.

Adjudicators in Drill Competitions:—Colonel M. Moore, C.B.; Captain Phillips and Captain White, D.S.O.

SPORTS COMMENCE AT 1 o'clock p.m. SHARP.

The Committee reserve the right to cancel or alter any of the events.

The decision of the Committee shall be final, and no appeal can be taken to a Court of Law.

PRICE OF PROGRAMME   1d.

"Connaught Telegraph," Castlebar."

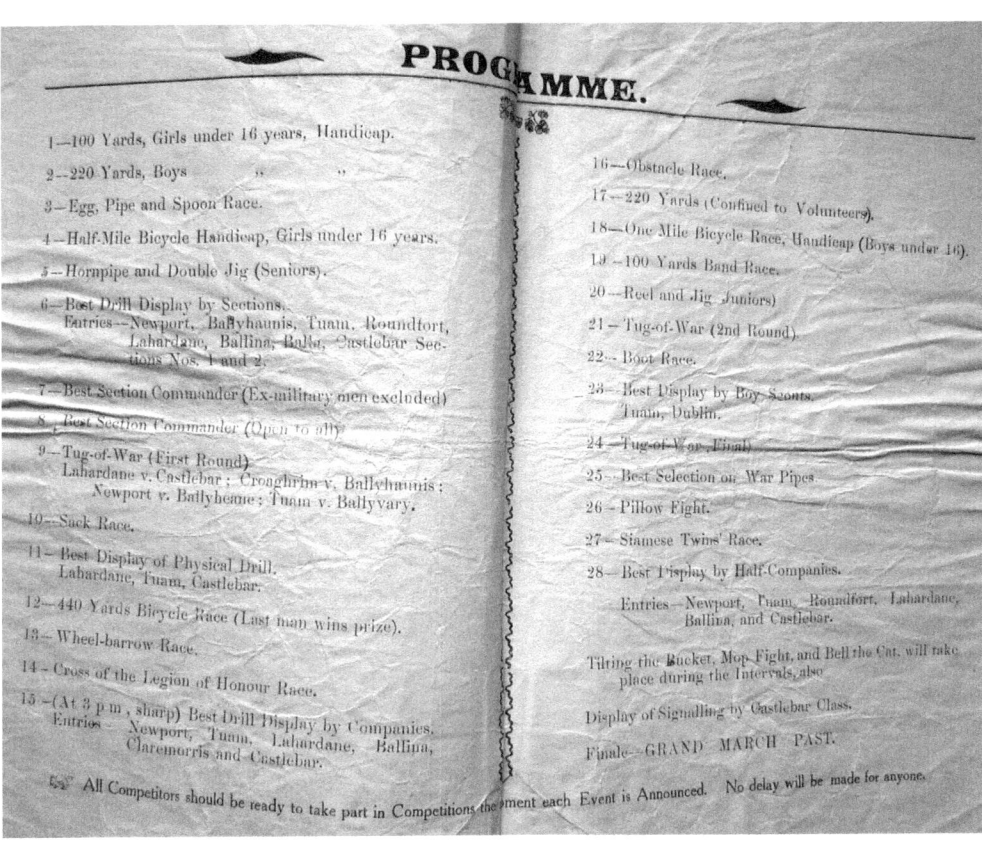

Sports day at the Mayo Lunatic Asylum in 1914. The Bureau of Military History has witness statements from the 1913-22 period, and Richard Walsh from Balla records that in the Autumn of 1920, the IRA held a convention under the cover of the asylum's Sports Day. (Courtesy of the National Library)

Opposite The Irish National Volunteers organised a sports day at the Mayo Lunatic Asylum in 1914. (Courtesy of the National Library)

The Lunatic Asylum had a staff band, as seen in this photo from the 1890s. (Courtesy of St Mary's/GMIT)

Staff at the Lunatic Asylum in the 1890s. (Courtesy of St Mary's/GMIT)

Staff at the Lunatic Asylum in the 1890s. (Courtesy of St Mary's/GMIT)

Staff at the Lunatic Asylum in the 1890s. (Courtesy of St Mary's/GMIT)

Staff at the Lunatic Asylum in the 1930s. (Courtesy of St Mary's/GMIT)

1971 nursing class in St Mary's Psychiatric Hospital (formerly called Mayo Lunatic Asylum). (Courtesy of GMIT – *Snapshots in Time*)

St Mary's Hospital, *c.* 1973. From left to right: Mary Mulchrone, Kathleen Moran, Mary Moran, Nellie Dunleavy. (Courtesy of St Mary's)

St Mary's Hospital day trip to Mulranny Beach, *c.* 1973. From left to right: Jerome Brennan, Willie Brehany, Mark O'Brien, Gus Moran, Paddy Cafferkey. (Courtesy of St Mary's)

St Mary's Hospital day trip to Mulranny Beach, *c.* 1974. From left to right: Sean Larkin, Annie Mae Ginty, Kathleen Gibbons, Sean Joyce. (Courtesy of St Mary's)

St Mary's Hall in GMIT today.

Castlebar Peace Park, opposite the fire brigade station, where thousands of deceased patients from Mayo Lunatic Asylum lie peacefully.

Another view of Castlebar Peace Park.

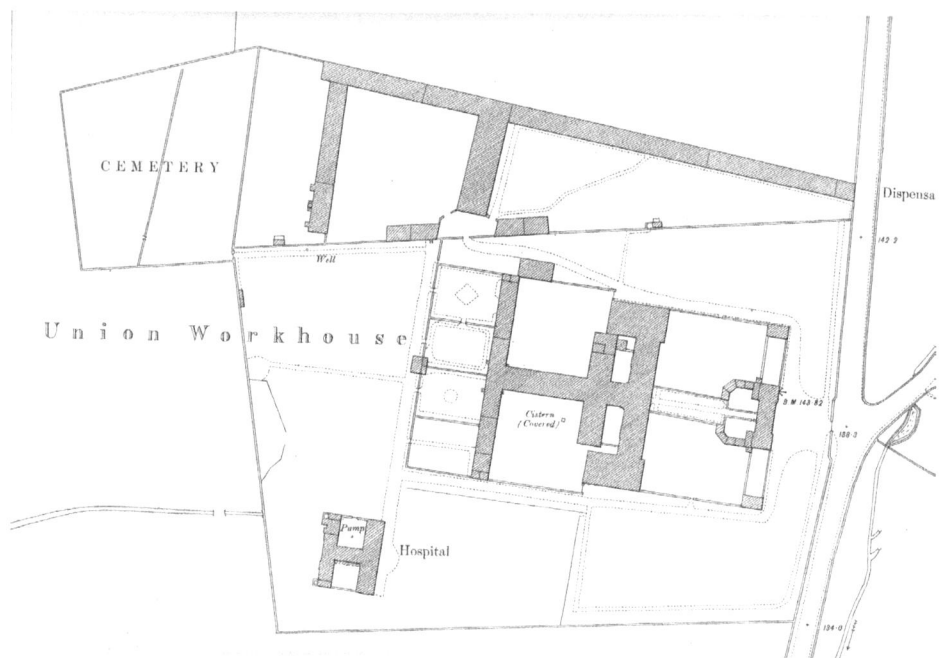

1893 Ordnance Survey map of the Workhouse, which was converted into the County Home in 1922. It was demolished in 1971 and a new Sacred Heart Home built on the site in 1973. The main buildings were in the centre, comprising a small admissions block nearest the public road, followed by the main accommodation block, and then an infirmary/'idiot's block' at the rear. The buildings to the right of the cemetery were auxiliary accommodation, built in 1850. The cemetery, with thousands of bodies, is still behind the Sacred Heart Home, although without any headstones or even a plaque. (Courtesy of Trinity College Dublin – Map Library)

The County Home around 1963 showing the front admissions block on the right and behind this, the taller accommodation block, with two gable roofs at each end. (Courtesy of Willie Jordan/*Castlebar Parish Magazine*)

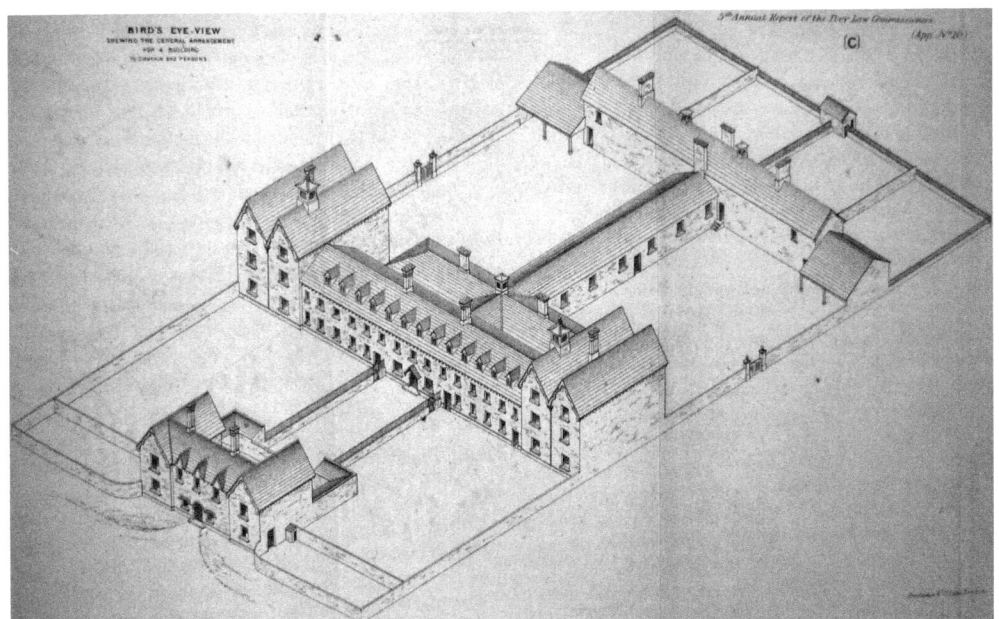

Most Workhouses in Ireland followed this layout: a small, attractive front admissions building; a central main building, with dormitories in the two gabled wings; then a chapel/dining room behind, leading to the infirmary/idiot's wards. (From 5th Annual Report of Poor Law Commissioners, 1839)

The County Home was formerly the dreaded Workhouse, and the gabled building on the right was the Admissions block. The buildings were demolished in the late 1960s and replaced by the Sacred Heart Hospital. (Courtesy of *Castlebar Parish Magazine*)

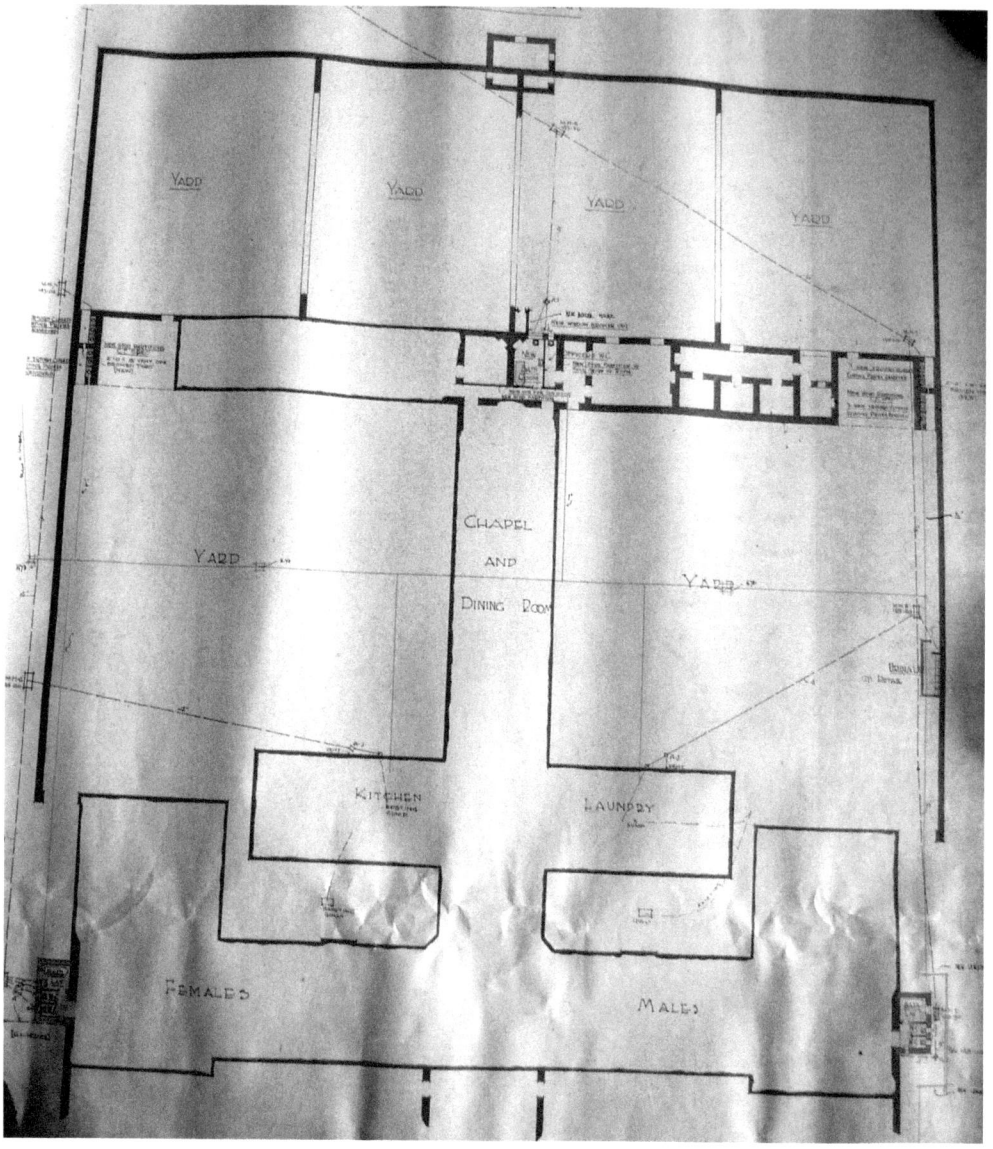

Toilets were added to Castlebar County Home in 1929. This plan shows the main accommodation block and the rear infirmary. Boys, girls, men, and women were in four separate sections, so that whole families were split up. The single-storey chapel-cum-dining room linked the main accommodation block with the rear infirmary. The little building at the top was the mortuary/dead house. (Courtesy of the Irish Architectural Archive)

In the old days, the main accommodation block would have been similar to how it is in this photo. The twin-gabled wings at each end were three storeys, while the main part was two-storey. The entire building only had two chimney stacks, meaning that those sleeping in the end wings nearly froze to death in winter.

This would have been a typical admissions building (although the single-storey wing on the right is a modern extension). The porter and probationary wards were located on the ground floor, with a boardroom for the occasional meetings on the first floor.

The two dormitories on the top floor in both the end wings would have been like this (minus the bit of modern insulation on the underside of the right-hand roof slope), with no fireplace. Even in the 1960s, some patients slept in accommodation not unlike this.

This would have been a typical narrow stone staircase at each end of the Workhouse.

In 1871, Miss Sarah Callaghan was the Matron of the Workhouse, on a salary of £30 a year, plus 8s 4d paid monthly in groceries. (Courtesy of the National Library)

Sacred Heart Home in modern times. From left to right, back row: Sally O'Malley, Noreen Donoghue, James Clarke, Goretti Brady, Archdeacon Con Heaney, Mary Kennedy, Sr Mary Teresa Johnston, Leonie Devereaux, Maura Collins, Sr Dominic Bryce. Front row: Flo Kearney, Kathleen Collins, Dr John Langan (medical officer), Sr Anthony Folliard (matron), Mary Monaghan (Assistant matron). (Courtesy of the Sisters of Mercy)

(E.)

CASTLEBAR UNION.

PERSONS who have Died in the Workhouse of the above Union from the 31st March 1850.

Number in Register.	NAME.	Age.	DATE of DEATH.	DISEASE.	Date of Admission to Workhouse.	
			1850:			
1,513	John Walsh	2	31 March	chronic dysentery	30 Aug. 1849	
573	Samuel M'Eneely	60	3 April	-- chronic bronchitis and anasarca.	10 Nov. —	
1,983	Martin Geraghty	9	3 —	chronic dysentery	19 Mar. 1850	
1,348	Margaret Fox	10	3 —	chronic dysentery	27 Sept. 1849	
1,294	Margaret Cavanagh	6	4 —	chronic dysentery	16 Aug. —	
333	John Brown	10	4 —	chronic dysentery	24 May 1847	
1,050	Mary Fox	10	5 —	chronic dysentery	17 Nov. 1849	
1,397	Honor Chambers	50	5 —	-- chronic dysentery and anasarca.	17 Nov. —	
769	David Henelly	3	6 —	-- chronic dysentery; sickly before admission.	11 Dec. —	
1,032	Pat. Moore	5	6 —	chronic dysentery	16 Aug. —	
534	Patrick Moran	8	6 —	chronic dysentery	11 Sept. —	
1,092	Mary Costello	8	8 —	-- chronic dysentery; disease before admission.	14 Feb. 1850	

Part of Appendix E of a government report by Captain Farren, dated 17 June 1850. In the six-week period in question, sixty-seven people died, as follows: John Walsh (aged 2), Samuel McEneely (60), Martin Geraghy (9), Margaret Fox (10), Margaret Cavanagh (6), John Brown (10), Mary Fox (10), Honor Chambers (50), David Henelly (3), Pat Moore (5), Patrick Moran (8), Mary Costello (8), Mary Carroll (8), Eliza Warderge (8), Mary Cauly (50), Thomas Corrigan (6), Mary Clarke (4), Biddy Thornton (2), Biddy Cauly (10), Martin Flannery (4), William Nolan (50), Myles Roach (20), Michael Corrigan (14), Thomas Nester (3), Edward King (49), Honor Foy (50), Thomas Madden (6), Mary Heneghan (16), Catherine Nolan (9), Sibby Browne (52), Biddy Connelly (58), Pat Hopkins (18), Michael Conlin (60), Biddy Jennings (6), Ellen Harding (10), Mary Chambers (20), George McNally (50), Anne Roache (9), Michael Devin (7), Sibby Moran (70), John Connor (10), William Mally (1), Biddy Carney (50), Martin Mulchrone (14), Biddy McFadden (10), John Foy (8), Michael Sheridan (15), Sibby Corrigan (50), James Kilcoyne (50), Michael Walsh (8), Catherine Gavan (10), Patrick Horan (6), Bridget Brogan (7), Bridget Geraghty (10), Pat Flannery (6), Anthony Kielty (10), Catherine McDonagh (60), John Noon (58), Michael Rafferty (10), David Crean (70), Sally Butler (6), Margaret Gorman (70), Bridget Quin (9), Mary Mally (16), Philip Davis (7), Biddy Gallagher (60), Mary Hughes (14). (Courtesy of DIPPAM – HC 1850 (461) 50 83)

It is doubtful if the 'last rites' were given to our ancestors, or if there were funeral Masses/services, prayers recited at the graveside, or even if the cemetery itself is 'consecrated ground'. Our 'loved ones' lie in an abandoned overgrown wasteland.

4

RELIGION AND EDUCATION

THE CHURCH OF THE HOLY ROSARY

The Church of the Holy Rosary is in the Diocese of Tuam and the parish of Agish, Ballyheane and Breaghwy. The old St Mary's church, dating from 1800, was to the east of the present building, and included a rear public gallery and organ loft. At the instigation of Archbishop Mc Hale, a new church was started in 1876, to a design by J.J. O'Callaghan, with funding from the diaspora in the USA. This church was on a higher site opposite the original church. Parish priest Canon Magee was halfway through the project when he died in 1885. His successor, Canon Lyons, demolished the half-completed church in 1891, much to the consternation of parishioners and donors, and built the present church alongside the old St Mary's church. Walter Doolin designed the present church, which was started in 1897 and opened in 1901. James Pearse, the English father of Padraig Pearse, made the marble altar, and the stained glass was by Meyer of Munich, Germany. The original design provided for a spire on top of the tower. A parochial house was built in 1904 on the site of the aborted church, although there is also a nearby presbytery dating from 1863. In 1986, the altar was turned around to face the people, following the Second Vatican Council in the 1960s.

CHRIST CHURCH

The Protestant church was built by the Anglicans in 1739, but was damaged during the uprising of 1798. A stone tablet in the cemetery records the date 1739, naming Sir John Bingham and John Edmondton as the first church wardens, Revd Thomas Ellison as the minister, Richard Castle (Cassels) as the architect, and T. Dickson as the builder. The church is described in Dr Pococke's *Irish Tour*, 1752: 'they have lately built a handsome church of Mr Castles design, it is the Greek Cross with three galleries: the windows and Cornish are of hewn lime stone which is the finest black marble,' – Greek crosses have four equal arms, unlike the Roman crucifixion cross.

The church archives note that the Easter Vestry met in the Methodist Church in 1824, and in the Courthouse in following years, because the congregation had no church. A new church was completed for about £2,500 on an extended site around 1830/31, with Mr Richards as the architect and Mr O'Connor from Sligo as the builder.

The organ was installed in 1904, as was the east window depicting the Ascension (by Mayer of Munich, Germany). The stained-glass window in the south transept dates from 1905, and is the work of the famous Sarah Purser of Dublin.

The tower has a two-faced clock, installed in 1904 by Smiths of Derby, England, and was gifted by the Brownes of Breaffy House. This is still hand-wound on a regular basis and utilises two small bells for quarter-hourly chiming, in addition to hourly striking. These bells were cast in 1904 by Taylor of Loughborough, England. There is also a large three-quarter ton bell in the tower, cast in 1902 by the Fountain Head Bell Foundry/Matthew O'Byrne in Dublin, but this is no longer rung.

The rector from 1790 to 1805 was Revd Thomas Ellison, and he was also the Land Agent for Lord Lucan. The adjacent Ellison Street commemorates him.

The large statue beside the railings nearest Ellison Street is of General George O'Malley, commemorating his exploits in battle across the globe, although his burial took place in 1847 in Murrisk Abbey near Louisburgh. This statue dates from around the time of his death.

METHODIST CHURCH

The Methodist Church on The Mall dates from 1785, and its first stone was laid by John Wesley, the English founder of Methodism. The rear part of the building was the house or manse for the preacher, but apparently was added about twenty years later. The stone plaque over the church door reads as follows:

> This chapel was built for the Methodists under the patronage of Charles, Lord Lucan. The Rev. John Wesley A.M. laid the first stone, May 21st 1785. And this stone which I have set for a pillar shall be Gods house. Genesis 28.22.

The church closed around 1960 and was leased to Mayo County Council. An Art Centre occupied the church from 1976 to 1986, but since 2002 it has been back in religious use by the Christian Fellowship.

The former Parochial Hall/Mall School is located near the Christian Fellowship church, beside Rock Square, and has been owned by Castlebar Boxing Club since the late 1980s. A stone plaque on the outside proclaims: 'From a child thou hast known the Holy Scriptures which are able to make thee wise unto salvation through faith which is in Christ Jesus' (2 Timothy 3.15 of King James Bible). In Griffith's Valuation in the middle of the nineteenth century, the premises is listed as the Church Educational Society school house.

PRESBYTERIAN CHURCH

The first Presbyterians came to this area in the middle of the nineteenth century to work on the estate of Colonel Robert Fitzgerald in Turlough. Their first meeting in 1854 was in the Courthouse in Castlebar, led by Mr Andrew Brown. In 1861, they purchased a site in Lower Charles Street for a church and manse (presbytery). The foundation stone was laid in 1863 by Henry Todd, of Todd Burns & Co. department store in Mary Street, Dublin (now Penneys). William Glanville was the architect. The church opened in November 1863, and Mr John Cairns was the first minister. The small, simple building has a depth equal to about one and a half times the width. A cottage around the corner in Richard Street was used as a school.

In 1924 the church, manse and school were sold to the Ryan family, and Nuala Armstrong (*née* Ryan) of Newtown still has fond memories of playing in the former church.

Nowadays the building is used by the Tulsi Indian restaurant, with a mezzanine floor for diners. The former manse (presbytery) has been divided into two houses.

DE LA SALLE BROTHERS

The De la Salle brothers arrived in Castlebar in 1888, and took charge of St Patrick's National School in Upper Chapel Street, which had just been built by the parish priest and had 189 boys on the roll book. Before that, the National School was sited across the road beside the Catholic chapel. The brothers built their monastery opposite the school in 1894. The National School was destroyed by fire in 1921, and again in 1956, after which the boys attended classes in the Military Barracks until a new school was completed in 1961. The building is now used as a HSE Family Centre, but there is a larger St Patrick's National School behind.

The brothers built St Gerald's Intermediate Technical School nearby in 1909, with an initial roll of twenty-four boys. They moved to a new building on the Newport Road in 1971, and the old college became the Parish Centre. The De la Salle order left the town in the year 2000, and the school is now run by lay people.

SISTERS OF MERCY

The nuns arrived in Castlebar in 1845 and acquired Grove House on Lower Charles Street, which they used as a private boarding school (Pension School) for a while. Through the good office of the parish priest, the nuns acquired Rock House off the Mall in 1853, for use as their convent, and converted an outhouse at the back into a National School. The chapel attached to the rear of the convent was built around 1854/55, followed by the formation of a nearby cemetery in 1857.

The convent was shown on the 1838 Ordnance Survey Town Plan as two distinct buildings, with the north one marked as a bank. The original property was leased in 1804 by the Earl of Lucan to Elizabeth Bourke, who sold it in 1852 to Revd James McHale for £1,375.

In 1897 the nuns built a new two-storey-over basement National School, St Angela's, in the middle of their back garden. In 1918, St Joseph's Secondary School was built in the space between the convent and the National School, and a north extension was added in the 1930s. To the east of St Angela's were the laundry, music room, toilets, and bicycle shed. The rear garden, which ran alongside the north-west of the Army Barracks, was used for growing vegetables and flowers, and included a glasshouse. A little stream ran along the north of the nun's property, and discharged into the nearby Castlebar River. Originally, the nun's garden extended only as far as the barracks entrance, but they acquired a large grove of trees at the north-west corner of the barracks at a later date.

In the 1901 census, the premises had thirty-one rooms and twenty-one nuns, including two aged 18 years, and four domestics. At the time of the 1911 Census, there is reference to their National School, and also a technical school. By now there are forty-eight rooms and nineteen nuns, including the Prioress Sr Margaret Fleming.

In 1924, just after the Civil War, the nuns bought The Lawn house and 92-acre demesne from Lord Lucan for £2,900. They converted the house into sleeping accommodation for boarders attending St Joseph's Secondary School beside the convent, and the farming activities were continued. The original Lawn house was gutted by a fire on the night of 25 October 1935, but thankfully none of the boarders were seriously injured. The Lawn was rebuilt not long after this.

Shortly after the fire a tunnel was built under the barracks road, to allow easier pedestrian access between The Lawn and the school/convent. In 1964, the nuns built a new St Angela's National School in the grounds of The Lawn, thereby allowing all the buildings attached to their old convent to be used as St Joseph's Secondary School.

A grotto to Our Lady stood against the gable wall of the chapel, where newly professed Children of Mary were photographed. Up until the 1970s, the nuns still ran a boarding school, with the young ladies living in the old Lawn house, from which they would walk across, via the tunnel, to St Joseph's Secondary School, wearing their bonnets. The Lawn had its own little chapel. In those years the nuns still wore the black-and-white full-length habit.

Up until the 1960s, all students up to Intermediate Certificate were taught in Irish. Mother Mary Agnes taught Irish, Sr Cecelia taught singing, Sr Perpetua taught Latin, 'Sponge' taught shorthand and typing, Sr Pius taught domestic science, and Mother Muradec from Ballina taught another, unspecified, subject. Oral Irish exams were held in the nun's lovely parlour.

The nun's chapel beside the convent was open to the public for Sunday Mass. Behind the elaborate marble altar, there were two narrow lancet windows with beautiful stained glass, and a six-sided circular window above these, also with stained glass.

In 1997, Sisters of Mercy (Tuam Diocese) Co. Ltd sold off their original Castlebar convent and secondary school (on a 2-acre site) for £420,000, to two men from Letterkenny, Co. Donegal. The original St Angela's National School is now the Social Services Centre (Meals-on-Wheels), funded by the HSE. The nuns exhumed the bodies from their cemetery and re-interred them in a plot in the public cemetery. The old convent, chapel and school were demolished in 2002, although the stained glass, marble altar, and other treasures were probably removed by the nuns at an earlier date and re-used in other convents.

The Lawn house had been extended in 1982 into a large secondary school, and nowadays caters for around 580 girls. The 1964 National School caters for 426 girls.

Since 2008, the nuns have lived in a large state-of-the-art convent on top of the hill overlooking their schools, called Ard Bhride Community, a retirement home for all Mercy convents in Mayo. The adjoining modern private nursing home, Cuan Chaitriona, caters for many infirm nuns, and was in fact originally built by the nuns.

OTHER SCHOOLS

The Taylor and Skinner road map of 1783 shows a Charter School, south of Christ Church. In a letter to John Hely Hutchinson, dated 17 April 1786, Lord Lucan states that he has established a school in Castlebar, paying the master £20 a year; about thirty boys attend. A government report of 1812 calls the latter a Classical School, by then closed.

The Second Report of the Committee of Public Instruction, dated 1835, records twelve schools in Castlebar. There was a boys National School and a girls National School, each with average daily attendance of 110 children. The rector funded a Protestant school, with about forty-five boys and thirty-five girls sharing the same building (the 1895 Ordnance Survey map shows Christ Church School on the site of the present Mayo County Library – this was probably previously called the Charter or Classical School). The other schools were small fee-paying ones.

The Vocational School opened in Newtown, near St Gerald's, in 1933, and Davitt College, another vocational school, opened in 1982.

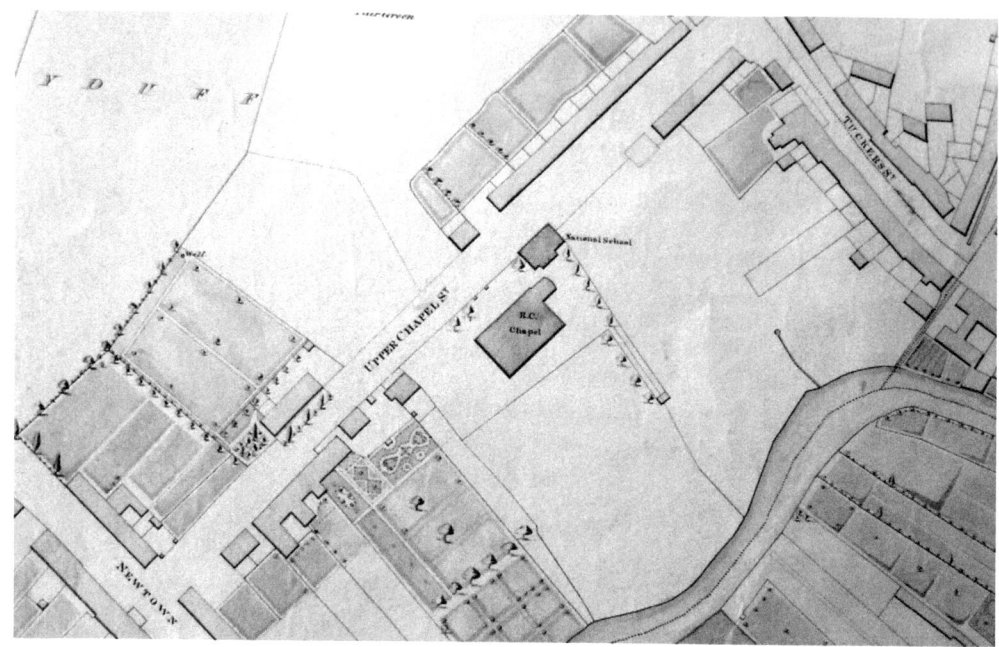

Upper Chapel Street on the 1838 Ordnance Survey Town Plan. The old St Mary's Chapel is the main feature, with the National School to its right. (Courtesy of the National Archives)

Map from around 1910, showing the old St Mary's Chapel, alongside the new Church of the Holy Rosary. By this time the old National School is gone and St Patrick's National School has been built across the road from the old chapel. Also, St Gerald's Technical/Intermediate School has been built to the right of St Patrick's. (Courtesy of the Valuation Office)

1893 Ordnance Survey map showing the outline of the aborted new Church of the Holy Rosary, which was demolished when it reached roof level and replaced by the parish priest's house. The two houses to the left of the aborted church were the Constabulary Barracks (RIC). St Gerald's Technical School is not yet built. Note the town gasworks in Newtown. (Courtesy of Trinity College Dublin – Map Library)

The old St Mary's Chapel alongside the newly opened Church of the Holy Rosary. The beautiful interior included an ornate ribbed and vaulted ceiling, and a fabulous carved hardwood reredos behind the marble altar. (Wynne Family Collection)

This was the architect's design for the new Church of the Holy Rosary, but the spire was never built, leaving an unfinished tower. Note St Patrick's National School on the left, and St Patrick's Monastery on the right. (From the *Irish Builder*, courtesy of Irish Architectural Archive)

A present-day view of the Church of the Holy Rosary, with unfinished tower.

The present interior of Christ Church, which was re-built in the late 1820s.

The interior of Christ Church looking west, 2012.

1914 — 1919

IN HONOUR
of those from this Parish who fell, and those who served in the Great War.

Killed

ANDREWS R.H.	Lieut. R.I.F.	McHOLME J.N.	Sergt. Conn.R.
BINGHAM D.C.	Lieut. C.G.	MORRISSON W.	R.N.V.R.
KINSMAN C.H.	Lieut. R.E.	NEELY D.	The Buffs.
KNOTT E.M.	Capt. R.A.F.	SNOOK E.L.	Conn.R.

Also served

BECKETT D.	Lt. Conn.R.	LARMINIE J.A.	Lt. D.C.O. Baluchis.	McKEE H.		Q.M.S. R.I.R.
BINGHAM Hon. Sir C.E.	Major Gen.	LUCAN G.C. Earl of	Brigadier Gen.	McKEE W.M.		R.A.M.C
BINGHAM Hon. Sir F.R.	Major Gen.	MORONY W.	Lt. R.Innis. Fus	McKEE W.M.		K.L.R.
BINGHAM H.F.	Lt. R.H.A.	MORRISON J.A.	Lt. R.Innis. Fus	MILLER J.		Conn. R.
BINGHAM G.C.P. Lord	Lt.C.G.	MURRAY W.	Lt. R.E.	PRESTON W.McC.D.		R.N.
BINGHAM Hon. L.E.	Capt. R.F.A.	BRABAZON T.G.N.	R.A.M.C.	PRESTON J.J.		R.A.S.C. M.T.
BINGHAM R.C.	Lt.Col. C.G.	ELLIOTT W.	E.Y.R.	PRESTON T.J.		R.I.F.
CHADWICK R.G.	Capt. K.L.R.	HEANEY J.	Q.M.S. Conn.R.	READ W.E.		R.G.A.
DIXON F.E.R.	Lt. M.C.,R.E.	JACKSON A.	R.M.L.I.	SHARPE W.G.		A.F.A.
GAHAN E.J.B.	Capt. R.A.S.C.	KEENAN J.	K.L.R.	WATSON E.A.		R.F.A.
KNOTT G.P.	Col. R.A.V.C.	KEENAN R.	K.L.R.	YOUNG F.J.		R.F.A.

YOUNG A.C. R.A.S.C.

ETHEL DIXON V.A.D.	FLORENCE MAC DOWELL V.A.D.	EMILY MORONY V.A.D.

First World War memorial inside Christ Church. Catholic comrades are not listed.

Inside the gates of Christ Church is the tombstone of the Scottish soldiers who died in 1798. The smaller stone slab was on the original 1739 church, listing the architect, wardens, etc.

The Bingham (Lucan) memorial on the rear wall of Christ Church.

The south elevation of Christ Church. Note the sandstone tracery to the south transept window, which contains Sarah Purser stained glass, and also the attractive lancet windows on the nave.

Present-day Christ Church. Note the red-bricked 1904 post office on the right.

The former Methodist church on The Mall, now used by Christian Fellowship. The west part was the manse for the preacher, and built about twenty-years after the church.

The north elevation of the former Methodist church, looking towards Rock Square.

The actual Mall (or promenade), leading from Rock Square and The Lawn residence of the Binghams, towards Christ Church. The former Methodist church is on the left, and their school is on the right (the latter now occupied mostly by Castlebar Boxing Club).

The former Methodist church is now occupied by Christian Fellowship, and is a big hit with the young people of Castlebar.

Lucan Street in bygone days, with the Presbyterian church at the far end, and the manse to the left of it. (Courtesy of Nuala Armstrong)

These days the former Presbyterian church is occupied by Tulsi Indian restaurant, and the former manse has been sub-divided into two dwellings.

St Patrick's National School on the left and St Gerald's Intermediate School on the right, 1930s. (Courtesy of De la Salle Archives)

President Hillery outside the Church of the Holy Rosary in 1988, for the De la Salle centenary, with the FCA Guard of Honour. St Patrick's National School and St Gerald's Secondary School are on the left. (Courtesy of Captain Mick Bohan, OC, 54 Reserve Cavalry Squadron)

The first group entering St Gerald's Intermediate College in 1909, with Br Damian Daly. From left to right, back row: A. Bourke, F. Cannon, T. Sheridan, C. Stenson, M. Gillan, J. Chambers, F. Horton. Middle row: L. Sheridan, E. Mullen, J. Moroney, M. Boland, J. Mulligan, J. Elliott, T. Keegan, M. Cannon. Front row: J. Bourke, F. Elliott, P. Lavelle, B. Bourke, V. Boland, W. Sheridan, P. Mongey, M. Moran. (Courtesy of St Gerald's College)

St Gerald's Leaving Certificate, 1931/32. From left to right, front row: M. Heverin, P. Moneley, J. Staunton, G. Brady, J. Kilroy, J. Fahey, J. Carney, M. Lynch. Middle row: P. McGough, J. Lally, H. Kenny, P. Concannon, M. Egan, A. Golden, M. Scahill, G. Prendergast. Back row: P. Holmes, P. Marley, T. Mulgrew, P. O'Gara, T. McGowan. (Courtesy of St Gerald's College)

St Patrick's in the 1930s. (Courtesy of Centenary Book 2009/De la Salle Brothers)

St Gerald's Intermediate Certificate 1957. From left to right, back row: B. Moylette, J. Golden, P. MacDonagh, J. Williams, F. Fadden, J. Daly, P. MacDonnell, J. Nestor, G. Mongan, L. Byrne. Middle row: J. Walsh, B. Doherty, O. Neary, J. Fadden, M. Cameron, R. McGuinness, J. Healy, M. Brady, B. Boyle, J. Sheridan, J. Kenny. Front row: R. MacGing, I. Browne, J. Lally, P. Kilgallon, P. Beirne, G. MacHugh, S. Corcoran, M. Flannelly, P. Heverin, M. Smith. (Courtesy of Centenary Book 2009/De la Salle Bros)

1988 centenary celebrations. From left to right, back row: Br Bernard, Br Denis, Br Imar, Br Stanislaus, Br Ailbe, Br Maurice. Front row: Br Silvester, Archbishop Cassidy, Br Phelan. (Courtesy of St Gerald's College)

At the 2000 unveiling of a De la Salle statue outside the former St Gerald's were past pupils who became priests. Standing, from left to right: Paddy Smyth, Tommy Murphy, Declan Carroll. Seated: Chas Guthrie, Michael Neary (now an archbishop), Sean Kilcoyne, P.J. Niland. (Courtesy of *Castlebar Parish Magazine*)

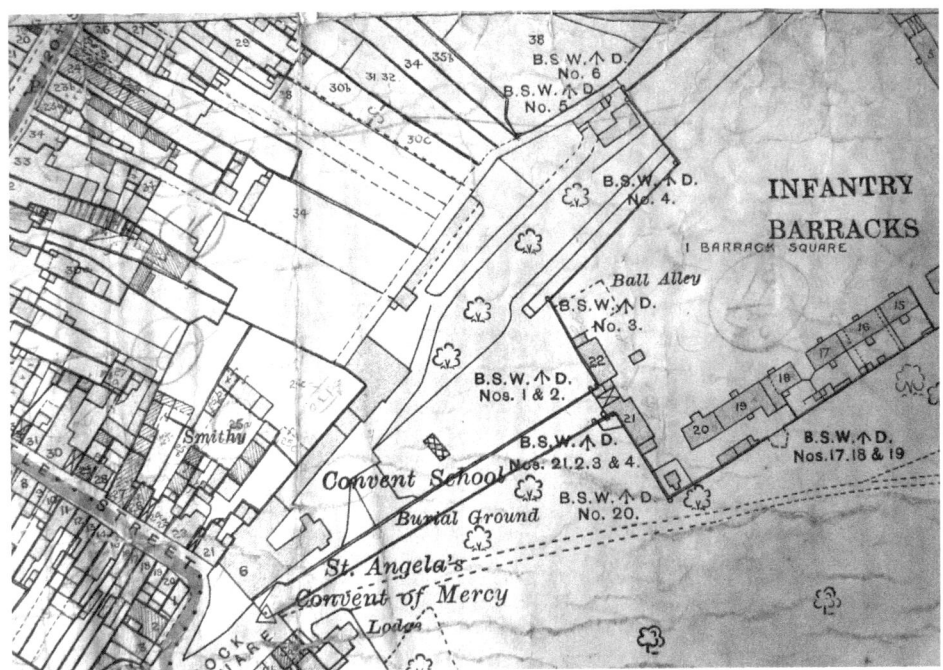

1910/20 map showing how the Mercy Convent jutted into the north-west corner of the Army Barracks. St Angela's National School is the L-shaped building about halfway down the garden. (Courtesy of the Valuation Office)

Modern aerial photo of part of the Mercy Convent. (Courtesy of the Sisters of Mercy)

Mercy Convent in January 2000 – notice the lovely cast-iron railings.

A present-day view of the Mercy Convent. All the beautiful and historic buildings are gone, except the former St Angela's National School.

The former St Angela's National School is now owned by the HSE, operating 'Meals-on-Wheels' for the elderly of Castlebar.

Recent view of the former St Angela's National School, as seen from the convent site. Note the archway at the end of the lane, leading into the Army Barracks. Many girls will remember the pedestrian tunnel under the lane, allowing access to The Lawn and the new schools.

Above Aerial photo showing the Mercy Convent at the bottom right-hand corner. The convent included the wooded area in their back garden, adjoining the Army Barracks. The Lawn can be seen in the centre at the top of the photo. (Courtesy of the National Library)

Left The Sisters of Mercy nuns had their own cemetery, which was transferred in recent years to the town's public facility. (Courtesy of the Sisters of Mercy)

Above Aerial photo of The Lawn (square building on right), by now St Joseph's boarding school. The left extension was built in 1982 and the rear extensions were in the course of construction at the time this photograph was taken. (Courtesy of the Sisters of Mercy)

Left The interior of the re-built Lawn today.

Pupils of St Angela's National School in the 1920s. (Courtesy of *Castlebar Parish Magazine*)

First-year students of St Joseph's Convent Secondary School in 1949. (Courtesy of *Castlebar Parish Magazine*)

Sr Consilio steers St Angela's National School confirmation class up McHale Road during a Corpus Christi procession in the 1960s. (Courtesy of *Castlebar Parish Magazine*)

St Joseph's and St Angela's school choir in the 1960s. (Courtesy of *Castlebar Parish Magazine*)

Sisters of Mercy, 1953, at the entrance to The Lawn. From left to right, back row: Clare Forde, Gabriel McLoughlin, Benignus Gibbons, Ann Neary, Vincent Fahy. Middle row: Agnes O'Rourke, Martha Hoban, Columba O'Flynn, Augustine Waldron, Kevin Casey, Cecelia Heslin, Alphonsus Mahon, Joseph Healy, Mercy Mooney, Patricia Galvin, Teresita Heraty, Evangelist Hennelly. Front row: Magdalen Naughton, Immaculata Hannon, Michael McDonagh, Sacred Heart Heverin, Muredech Harte, Lawrence Garvey, Peter Tiernan, Perpetua Cannon, Consilio Coyne. (Courtesy of the Sisters of Mercy)

1953 centenary celebrations in front of the Mercy Convent. (Courtesy of *Castlebar Parish Magazine*)

Sisters of Mercy nuns, c. 1980. From left to right, back row (standing): Ignatius Sheerin, Attracta Canney, Teresita Heraty, Mary Hennelly, Mary Johnson, Maire Naughton, Baptist McEvilly (Xavier), Mary Feeney. Front row: Vincent Fahy, Magdalen Naughton, Alacoque Lowry, Laurence Garvey, Genevieve Nolan, Agnes O'Rourke. (Courtesy of the Sisters of Mercy)

Interior of Mercy Convent chapel. (Courtesy of the Sisters of Mercy)

Sr Geraldine with the 1977 First Holy Communion class in St Angela's National School. (Courtesy of *Castlebar Parish Magazine*)

1992 Leaving Certificate class in St Joseph's gym. (Courtesy of Grace O'Malley – photographer unknown)

5

BUSINESS

In the eighteenth century, linen-making from flax grown in the fields around Castlebar was widespread. In 1776, Arthur Young wrote that there were about 200 looms in Castlebar, with weavers working from their homes in Tucker Street and New Antrim Street. In 1790, Lord Lucan built the Linenhall as a market for the weavers' produce.

The Statistical Survey of 1802 records: 'Three bleach-mills about Castlebar, one good flour-mill, beside a great number of common oat and tuck-mills.' Tuck mills were associated with the linen industry, and were engaged in cleaning cloth and making it thicker. The survey, under the heading of 'Manufacturers', then says: 'The linen manufacture is in this barony (Barony of Carra) arrived at a high degree of improvement, and has been, by pains and improvements, brought to its present perfection by the late Lord Lucan. Here is at Castlebar a linen-hall, where upwards of five hundred pounds are laid out every Saturday.' By the time of Griffith's Valuation in the 1850s, the Linenhall was unoccupied.

From the late 1890s the Catholic Church used the Linenhall as a social centre, with clubs, concerts, etc., calling it the Town Hall. Since 1986 the building has been used as the Linenhall Arts Centre.

CASTLEBAR AIRPORT

Castlebar Airport on Breaffy Road was opened in 1966 by brothers Peter, Hugh, James, and Joseph Ryan, and their brother-in-law Dermot McDermott of Castlerea, Co. Roscommon. Michael Heverin joined the company in 1969. The set-up costs included £4,500 for the site, £23,000 for the runway, and £7,500 for the terminal building. The runway was 2,000ft long and 70ft wide, and the 13-acre site was originally part of the farm attached to St Mary's Psychiatric Hospital. The aeroplanes using the facility varied from two to ten-seaters, including the Beagle 206, the Aztec, the Beech Baron, and the Islander. Another local group, called Ireland West Airlines Ltd, operated a charter service using a Piper Cherokee-Six from 1968. The Castlebar Air Show was a popular attraction, and the airport bar was also a venue for parties. The airport closed in 2001.

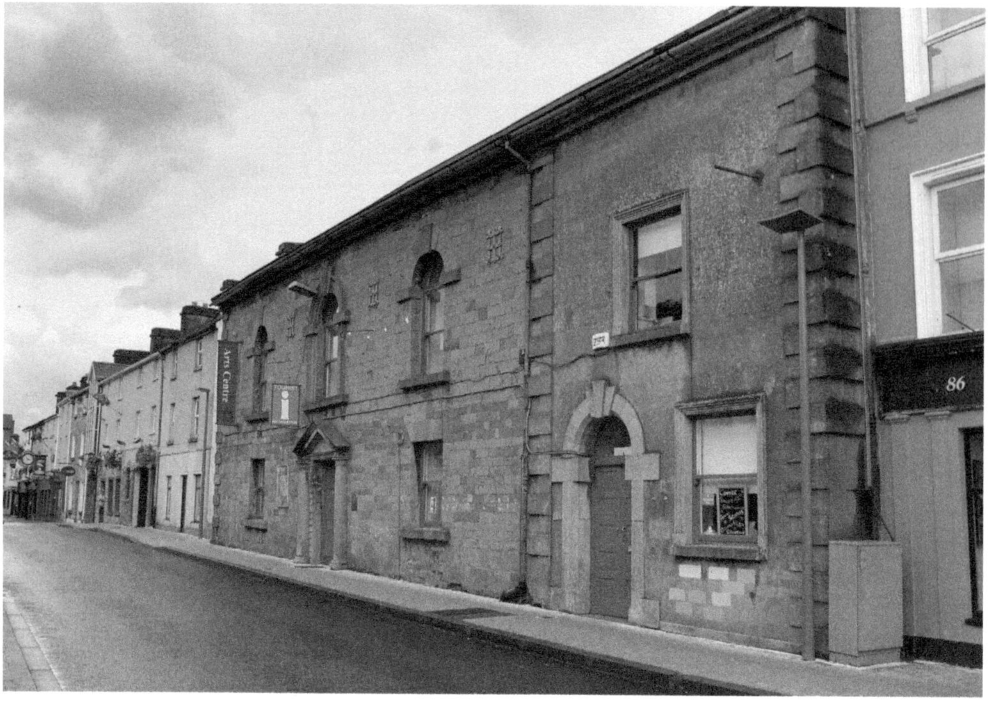

The Linenhall is now an arts centre, café, tourist office and concert hall.

CASTLEBAR AIRPORT CO. LTD.
CASTLEBAR,
CO. MAYO,
IRELAND.

Telephone 448

9th April, 1969.

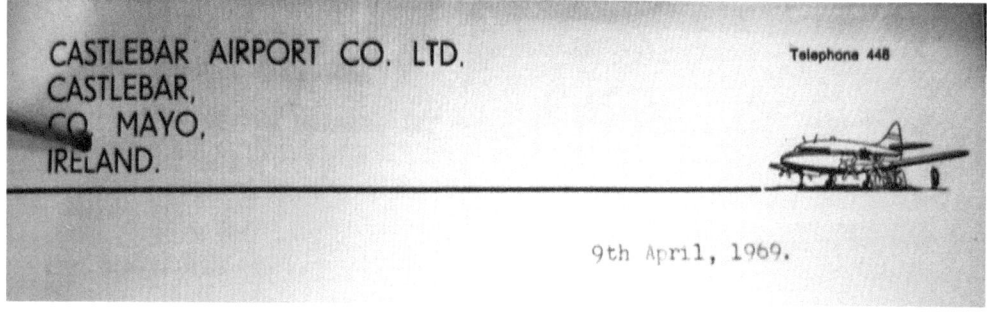

Company headed paper. (Courtesy of the Companies Registration Office)

The former Castlebar Airport. (Courtesy of *Castlebar Parish Magazine*)

Another view of the former Castlebar Airport. (Courtesy of *Castlebar Parish Magazine*)

The former airport terminal in 2001. It has since been developed as the Castlebar Retail Park, with retail outlets such as Woodies.

Travenol Laboratories Ltd (from Chicago) was completed in 1972, at a cost of £630,000. The fully air-conditioned, single-storey building occupied about 7,000m^2 (roughly 75,000ft^2), and was extended within a few years by another 9,300m^2 (100,000ft^2). Now called Baxter Healthcare, it is the biggest employer in Castlebar. Note the adjoining Castlebar Airport and runway. (Courtesy of Baxter Healthcare)

CASTLEBAR BACON FACTORY

Castlebar Bacon Factory was sited on the McHale Road, from 1917 to 1989, and was famous for 'Barcastle' sausages and pudding, and also tinned meat. They had their own slaughterhouse on site, and also a poultry section, and a shop at the entrance. McHale Road houses were built in the 1930s and many occupants worked in the factory.

The original business was called the Castlebar Co-Operative Bacon Curing Factory, and was located in the extensive farmyard of The Lawn. In the early years, the manager was J.E. Prossor, the chairman was Mr Larminie, JP, while the managing director was Brian van Zwanenberg of London. In the 1930s and 1940s, Mr Hartog Salamon de Jong, from Holland, was the managing director. In 1962, Mr van Zwanenberg was chairman and he reported that 5,325 tons of meat were being exported, mostly through Dublin Port. The directors in the 1960s included Brendan Sheary, James McKernan, and Colm Fay. By 1973 the turnover was £4.2m, and the chairman was J.F. Clarfelt. In 1975, Blair Hold was the manager and by 1977 the turnover was £9.5m.

The Boning Hall was officially opened in 1958 by the Taoiseach, Sean Lemass, and blessed by Fr Alfred Fair. The factory is now all gone, except for the Canning building, which has been converted into small industrial units (located opposite the Hogs Heaven pub). The new retail park on the site is called Barcastle. The 1954 statue of Our Lady was relocated when the bypass was built in the 1990s, and is now positioned at the top of McHale Road.

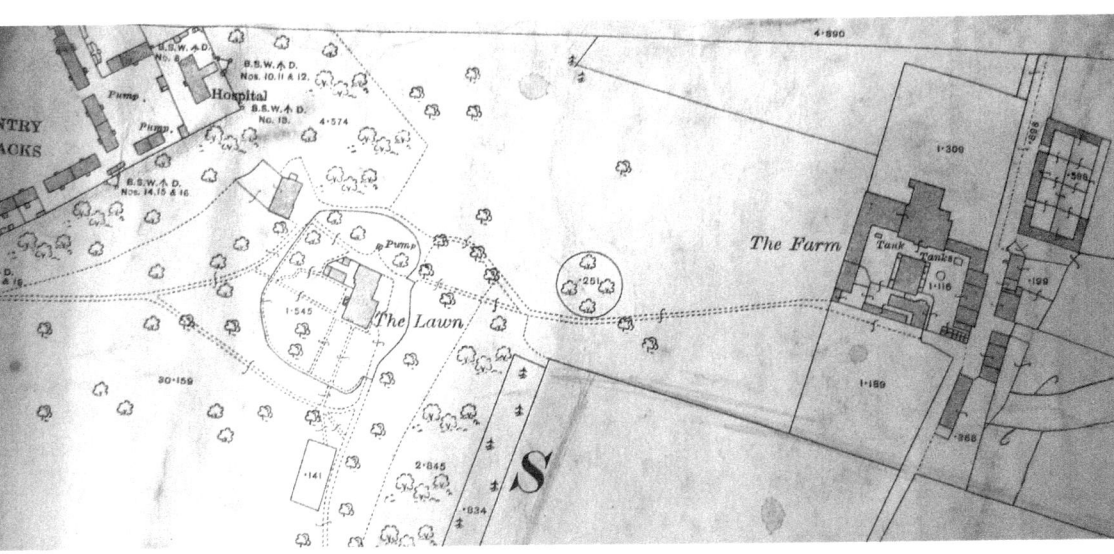

The farm was the farmyard of The Lawn in the time of the Binghams/Lord Lucan. In 1917, the farm was sold to businessmen, who set up the Bacon Factory here. (Courtesy of the Valuation Office)

Sketch of Castlebar in 1880, by C.W. Cole, when pigs were pets. (Courtesy of the National Library)

Aerial view of the extensive Bacon Factory buildings at the end of McHale Road. (Courtesy of the Hogs Heaven pub, which is now in the same location)

Close-up of the Bacon Factory. (Courtesy of the Hogs Heaven pub)

The iconic blue and white 1954 Marian Shrine outside the entrance to the former Bacon Factory was recently moved and re-erected to allow construction of the new bypass. Barcastle Business Park has now been built on the old factory site.

Plenty of 'back rashers' in this one! (Courtesy of the Hogs Heaven pub)

A more modern view of the Bacon Factory canteen. (Courtesy of the Hogs Heaven pub)

Bacon Factory fleet of vans. (Courtesy of *Castlebar Parish Magazine*)

Spencer Park – a 14½-acre estate with a three-bay, two-storey house – was sold by the Landed Estates Court in 1858, at which stage it was occupied at an annual rent of £110, under an 1838 lease between Major Owen O'Malley and John C. Larminie. In turn, O'Malley had a ground lease from the Earl of Lucan. The estate gave the name to Spencer Street. (Postcard from the Local History section in Mayo County Council Library)

The County Cinema was started by Gussie Bourke in 1939 in Spencer Street. It was burned down in 1948 and reopened in 1949, with a capacity of 640. It closed in 1999, when it was a twin-cinema. In the 1920s, there was the Ellison Cinema in Ellison Street. (Tom Campbell photo supplied by Failte Ireland)

Daly's Imperial Hotel on The Mall is reputed to have been founded in 1785 as a coaching inn, where the Mail Coach stopped. There is no mention of this hotel in *Slaters Commercial Directory* of 1846, and instead, Foys Hotel in Ellison Street is listed as a Mail Coach stop. Mary Harton was the owner in 1901, then Robert Read in 1911; the Pelly family operated the hotel for many decades thereafter. The Mayo Land League was founded in 1879 in Daly's Hotel by the then owner James Daly, and Michael Davitt. The League later became a nationwide organisation. This photograph was taken in 2009, before the County Council bought the premises – it now stands vacant.

The O'Malley family in Daly's Hotel's famous panelled dining room, January 2000. From left to right: Grace, Martin, Joanne, Matt, Pauline, Mark.

The Mall around 1900, with the Methodist church on the left, Daly's Hotel in the centre, and a bank on the right. (Courtesy of the National Library – Lawrence Collection)

Imperial Hotel in the mid-twentieth century. (Courtesy of Local History section in Mayo County Council Library)

WESTERN HATS

The government sent a trade mission to France in the bleak 1930s and persuaded some Jewish businessmen to set up factories in the west of Ireland – Hirsch Ribbons in Longford, 'Les Modes Modernes' in Galway, and Western Hats. The latter opened in Castlebar on the Newport Road in 1939, lasting until the 1970s and employing about 150 people at its height. It was owned by a Belgium company and was initially managed by Franz Schmolka, although over the years many local people acquired shares in the company, and the final directors were all Irish.

The first directors in April 1939 were: Edmond Claessens of Verviers, Belgium; Franz Schmolka, a Belgian living in 22 Pembroke Park, Dublin (he is later listed as a native of Czechoslovakia); Marcus Witztum, an Austrian living in Rathfarnham, Dublin; and Senator Sean McEllin of Brize House, Claremorris. Edouard Zurstrassen from Belgium joined the Board in May 1939. Marcus Witztum was also a director of Les Modes Modernes and Viennese Knitted Goods Co. Ltd. The original company was called Castle Hat Co. Ltd, but changed its name to Western Hats Ltd in 1939.

The initial paid-up share capital was £19,473. Lake Lawn, comprising 9½ acres, was bought for £1,700 in 1939 from Alice Quinn of Ellison Street. Joseph Leclercq of Belgium built the factory for £6,100 – the concrete roof is of north-light configuration, to receive the maximum amount of daylight during the long winter months. Some factory workers were sent for training in Verviers, Belgium. Walter Porges was general manager and a director in the 1960s. Blackfort on the Newport Road became the Jewish quarter of Castlebar, since about a dozen families came from Europe to manage and work in the factory. The factory range included 'Stetson hats' for men, as well as the caps and hats worn by every man in that era. Women usually wore scarves on their heads, especially in church, so there was no business in that field, but they did make berets for the army.

Machinery was steam powered, with the big landmark brick chimney serving the boiler. The factory hooter, signifying start and finish of work, lunch break, etc., could be heard over a wide area. Around 1972, part of the premises was used by Gumbacher (makers of art materials), and around 1976 Rehab occupied another part. The hat factory was sold to the Rehab institute in 1981, who stayed until 2003 before moving to a new building on Breaffy Road. The factory now lies substantially derelict, and the landmark brick chimney has gone.

Aerial photo of Castlebar in 1972, with the hat factory in the lower right-hand corner. (Courtesy of the National Library)

Staff photo outside Western Hats, and only two hats in sight! (Courtesy of Nuala Armstrong/ *Castlebar Parish Magazine*)

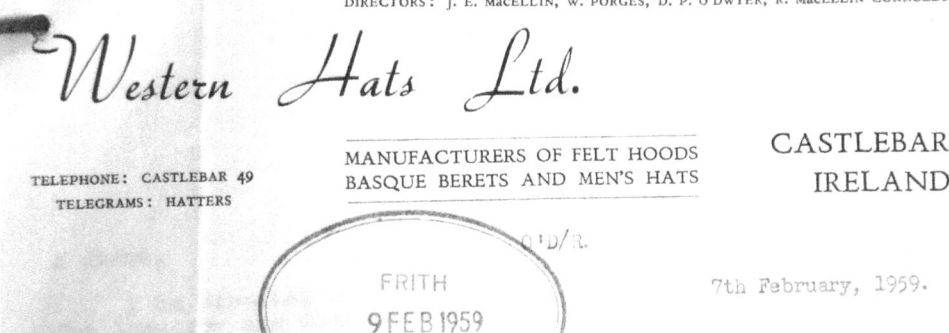

Company headed paper. (Courtesy of the Companies Registration Office)

Staff from Western Hats display their wares in the St Patrick's Day Parade in Castlebar. (Courtesy of Nuala Armstrong/*Castlebar Parish Magazine*)

Western Hats. (Courtesy of Nuala Armstrong)

Western Hats in 1948. From left to right: Betty Corcoran, Katie Moran, Andy Leonard, Josie Hopkins, Bridie O'Shaughnessy. (Courtesy of *Castlebar Parish Magazine/Connaught Telegraph*)

Western Hats. (Courtesy of Nuala Armstrong/Albany Home Decor)

Two lovely ladies wrap and pack the felt products in the hat factory. (Courtesy of the *Connaught Telegraph*/*Castlebar Parish Magazine*)

Staff of the hat factory enjoy a night out in the late 1950s. (Courtesy of the *Connaught Telegraph/Castlebar Parish Magazine*)

The former hat factory is still standing, but mostly empty, and the landmark brick chimney is gone.

The hat factory was built in 1939. It was built to last, being made entirely of in situ reinforced concrete.

Even the north-light roofs of the factory were made of insitu reinforced concrete.

Josie Bourke's garage, Ellison Street, now John O'Donnell Chemist and Mongey Opticians. Joseph Burke moved in the 1960s to Market Square. (Courtesy of *Castlebar Parish Magazine*)

The junction of Ellison Street and The Mall, 1948. Burleigh House on the left, followed by Josie Bourke's garage, *Connaught Telegraph* building, Chambers House (former RIC Barracks), and the bank. (Courtesy of Bord Failte)

Ellison Street, c. 1930. (Postcard courtesy of Local History section, Mayo County Council Library)

Ellison Street in the late 1950s, with Josie Bourke's garage on the left. (Postcard courtesy of Local History section, Mayo County Council Library)

Present-day Ellison Street, with the imposing Burleigh House on the left. Permanent TSB has been rebuilt, formerly the *Connaught Telegraph* building, and a storey higher.

Present-day Ellison Street looking towards Christ Church. Note the three-storey Chambers House on the right, which was a former RIC Barracks.

The Upper Crust Lavelles Bakery. This family have been doing business in Castlebar for around 175 years, and have been located in Bridge Street since 1904, when they were also known as the Riverside Bakery.

The single-storey Xtra-Vision shop was built in 1925, directly over the River Castlebar.

The nineteen-century buildings of Lavelles Bakery were built in two phases, with the north block added later in the century. They are still standing, although not in use.

Lavelles Bakery, with the Church of the Holy Rosary and the former St Patrick's National School in the background.

Early twentieth-century view of Ellison Street. (Postcard courtesy of Local History section, Mayo County Council Library)

Ellison Street, *c.* 1890-1910. The blurred image in the centre shows a donkey with cleeves of turf. (Courtesy of the National Library – Lawrence Collection)

Gavin's grocery store, Spencer Street, in January 2000.

Tom and Luke McHugh opened the Welcome Inn hotel in 1962. (Courtesy of the McHugh family)

The post office on Ellison Street dates from 1904, and was designed by J.H. Pentland, who later worked for the Board of Works. Prior to that, the post office was beside the Cavalry Barracks (now the Garda station), where soprano Margaret Burke Sheridan lived. This photo shows the staff in 1911. The sorting office closed in 2012 and moved to Quarryfield Business Park. (Courtesy of *Castlebar Parish Magazine*)

  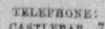

The Connaught Telegraph
ESTABLISHED 1828.

The oldest and best Advertising Medium in the Province.

Ellison Street,
Castlebar.
Co. Mayo.
18th August 1953

Office of the President
Arus an Uachtarain,
Phoenix Park,
Dublin

The *Telegraph or Connaught Ranger* newspaper was founded on St Patrick's Day, 1828, by the Nationalist Frederick Cavendish, and was renamed the *Connaught Telegraph* in the 1870s. James Daly was editor at the time of the founding of the Land League in Daly's Hotel in 1879. The Gillespie family are the current owners, going back many generations. The paper was based at the corner of Cavendish Lane and Ellison Street for years, but the building was demolished in 1996 to make way for the new Permanent TSB premises, and the newspaper moved to a new building in Cavendish Lane. (Courtesy of the National Archives)

Castle Street in the days when the bicycle ruled the road. Note the tall Mercy Convent on the right. (Postcard courtesy of Local History section, Mayo County Council)

Castlebar Gas Co., based in Newtown, closed in 1913. The town got electric lighting in 1916, operated by J. Bourke & Sons of Ellison Street. The new power plant was on the north side of Market Square, opposite the old gasworks. Note the presbytery in the background. (Courtesy of Local History section, Mayo County Council Library)

Fahey's gift shop, Main Street, was called Geevy's Hotel at the time of the 1798 uprising. Various businesses, including the Star Picture Palace for a few years around 1919 (at the rear of Connaught Cycle Works), were in occupation, until the building was bought in 1954 by the Fahey family, who are still there. (Courtesy of Mary Fahey)

Present-day Castle Street. Note the balls on the pillars at the entrance to the barracks, and the absence of the Mercy Convent. The former Erris Hotel is halfway down on the left side. Parsons Shoes are on the left of this photo.

Staball Hill, also known as Poor House Hill, was the reputed entry point for General Humbert's men in 1798. St Angela's Girls National School can be seen at the back left, and Christ Church pinnacles at the back right. (Courtesy of the National Library – Lawrence Collection)

Castlebar railway station opened in 1862 and was a long way from the town centre back then. This photo is from around 1880 and shows a steam engine at the station. (Courtesy of the National Library – Wynne Collection)

THE BREWERY

There was once a brewery in Ellison Street, opposite Christ Church. The 9-acre vacant property was sold in 1858 by the Landed Estates Court as a development opportunity. The Conditions of Sale stated that the premises were held under lease dated 7 September 1700, between Sir John Bingham, Baronet, and James Clarke, the ancestor of Owen O'Malley. One of the lease covenants required the tenant to grind any corn grown on the premises at the mill of Ballynew. The former brewery and malthouse were towards the rear of the site, beside the orchard, and the river and the field was let yearly to Revd William Stoney, the rector.

THE TRAVELLERS FRIEND HOTEL

Travellers Friend Hotel was opened in 1955 by the Jennings family; the site is now a major hospitality and entertainment venue called TF Royal.

WYNNES NEWSAGENT

Wynnes newsagent in Main Street started in 1837, and later branched into photography. Today, their historic collection of photographs of Mayo life is a national treasure.

The Breaffy House Hotel dates from around 1890, replacing an older house, and was designed by the architect William Fawsett for the Browne family. The Lee family converted it into a hotel in 1963. Following a fire, the hotel was rebuilt and extended in 1969 and the Jennings Group bought the hotel in 1984.

Aerial photo of Castlebar Airport, including the runway, with various small aircraft parked. The Travenol factory is directly opposite the airport, the latter being very useful for visiting American executives. (Courtesy of Roads Design, Mayo County Council)

Lough Lannagh, amidst lush green pastures, is now a wonderful amenity enjoyed by Castlebar residents and visitors. Note the ultra-modern exercise machine beside the shingle walking path.

Until recently, Lough Lannagh was overgrown and unknown to the people of Castlebar. Now the lake has tarmac paths all around, a pedestrian bridge, a central car park, exercise equipment, and a popular holiday village, making it the major centre of attraction in Castlebar. The photo shows the lake at dusk, with Croach Patrick in the distance.

OTHER BOOKS BY THE AUTHOR

Harold's Cross In Old Photographs

Mount Merrion In Old Photographs

If you enjoyed this book, you may also be interested in ...

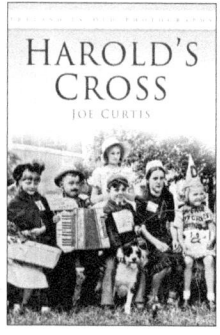

Harold's Cross In Old Photographs

JOE CURTIS

Today Harold's Cross is a bustling thoroughfare, and although it is now a suburb on the south side of Dublin, it was once akin to the best little town in Ireland, being completely self-sufficient, with schools, churches, shops, pubs and many farms and orchards. For its residents, it has a rich and varied history, which is beautifully captured in this book of archive photographs.

978 1 84588 702 5

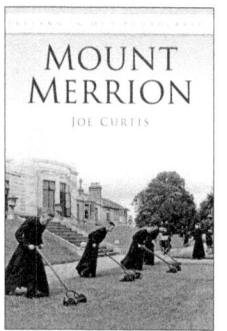

Mount Merrion In Old Photographs

JOE CURTIS

Mount Merrion lies on the south side of Dublin, 'between the mountains and the sea'. In 1711, the Fitzwilliam family walled the area to serve as their private country estate, and the 300th anniversary of this has sparked a new and enthusiastic interest in the history of the area. The early days of rustic open fields and tree-lined lanes are still in evidence, and this book by local historian and long-time Mount Merrion resident Joe Curtis continues that celebration.

978 1 84588 747 6

Rathmines In Old Photographs

MAURICE CURTIS

In his latest book, writer and historian Maurice Curtis takes the reader on a visual tour of Rathmines through the decades, recounting both the familiar and the forgotten, those features and events that may have faded over time. From the Battle of Rathmines in the seventeenth century (that changed the course of Irish history) to the achievements of Irish Independence and beyond in the twentieth century, Dr Curtis charts the development of this nationally important suburb that mirrors the changing face of Ireland itself.

978 1 84588 704 9

Portobello In Old Photographs

MAURICE CURTIS

In this book, Maurice Curtis, takes the reader on a visual tour of Portobello through the decades, recounting both the familiar and the events and places that have faded over time, revealing many fascinating details, including the fact that Dublin's Portobello was named after an area on the East Coast of Panama! This, and much more, is captured in a timeless volume, which pays fitting tribute to this well-loved part of the city.

978 1 84588 737 7

Visit our website and discover thousands of other History Press books.

www.thehistorypress.ie